The Josep.
Institute for Israel Studies
University of Maryland

MW01590899

Israel's Geopolitical Dilemma
And the Upheaval in the Middle East

Shlomo Hasson

2013

ISRAEL 2023 (2)

Israel's Geopolitical Dilemma
And the Upheaval in the Middle East

Shlomo Hasson

Translation from Hebrew: Mairav Zonszein

Cover Photo: Bünting, H., Itinerarium Sacre Scipturae. Helmstadt, Jacobus Lucius, 1585

ISBN 978-0-615-68565-6

What will Israel's geopolitical position be in 2023?

There are not many countries in the world like Israel, whose character, fate and very existence are so closely related to and embroiled in international politics. Its very establishment was largely dependent on a decision made by the United Nations and, today, the need for international legitimacy continues to be a necessary part of sustaining its existence. Of course, it is not solely this small country but the entire region that has, since ancient times, been the epicenter of friction between world powers which have determined its fate. Any forecast of Israel's future thus requires an examination of broader global processes.

It may have appeared as if the collapse of the Soviet Union put an end to the lengthy bipolar conflict of the twentieth century (a war that was not limited to being "cold"). However, now Israel finds itself positioned on the new borderline between the West and the awakening Muslim world. This phenomenon is just one aspect of the turbulent Middle East that emerged at the start of this decade and which, at its inception, became known as the "Arab Spring," still lacking a better, more permanent name.

As we enter the third year of this new era, Syria is embroiled in a vicious civil war, the internal struggle over Egypt's character continues, Jordan's Hashemite Kingdom is weakening, tensions between Shi'ites and Sunnis are deepening everywhere, and the possibility of a nuclear Iran hovers over it all. The situation is unpredictable, dynamic, and saturated with dangers and challenges.

For this reason, any attempt to assess how Israel will look when it celebrates its 75th birthday in 2023 cannot concentrate solely on internal processes, social divides, and political disputes; nor only on the struggle between the "Lexus advocates" and the "olive tree loyalists" – in other words, between those Israelis who want to see the country integrated into the processes of globalization and those who wish to preserve it as distinct, unique, and separate.

Attempting to determine what Israel's future holds thus requires the amalgamation of three dimensions (or sets of processes); namely, global, regional, and internal, beginning with the external processes. This booklet tackles all three of these dimensions in order to better assess Israel's geopolitical situation in 2023. While we cannot see into the future, we can project future scenarios by examining the most relevant forces and estimating which scenarios are more likely to take place.

This is the second publication in a series of comprehensive studies, written by Professor Shlomo Hasson from the Hebrew University Jerusalem, that comprise the Israel 2023 project, initiated by the Gildenhorn Institute for Israel Studies at the University of Maryland. Since its inception in 2006, the Institute has become one of the fastest-growing and highest profile centers for Israel studies in the United States. Last year 500 students enrolled in 15 different Israel Studies courses, ranging from history to politics to the Israeli-Palestinian conflict to Israeli society, culture, economics, and more.

The Institute also initiates and supports research on Israel and is home to the Israel Studies Review, the official journal of the Association for Israel Studies, an international scholarly organization. Located right next door to the American capital, the Gildenhorn Institute is able to make a significant contribution to the public and political discourse on Israel and the Middle East . To read more about the Institute and its activities, please go to www.israelstudies.umd.edu

The first booklet in the Israel 2023 series has already been published in both English and Hebrew and disseminated in Israel and the U.S. It examines future scenarios in the relations between Arabs and Jews in Israel and presents three distinct future possibilities: The "Confrontation Scenario," the "Liminal Scenario" and the "Reconciliation Scenario." The booklet may be accessed at www.israelstudies.umd.edu/Israel2023.html

The second booklet, "Israel's Geopolitical Dilemma and the Upheaval in the Middle East", was published in Hebrew at the start of the 2012 academic year, and the English version will be published early in 2013. The third and final booklet in the series, addressing the relationship between religion and state (and between religious and secular Jews) as Israel approaches 2023, will also be published in both languages.

This research project has been coordinated and written by Professor Shlomo Hasson, Director of the Shasha Center for Strategic Studies at the Hebrew University Jerusalem. Professor Hasson is an internationally renowned expert in the field of system analysis, specializing in the scenarios method, such as, for example, his study on the future of Jerusalem, which was well received in Israel and throughout the world. The purpose of this booklet and the others in the series is to promote public debate among public-opinion shapers, and especially among decisions-makers, who can directly impact the direction Israel chooses to go. Hopefully, they will succeed in making the right decisions.

Yoram Peri
Abraham S. and Jack Kay Chair in Israel Studies
Director of The Joseph and Alma Gildenhorn
Institute for Israel Studies
University of Maryland

TABLE OF CONTENTS

List of Illustrations

INTRODUCTION

Israel's major geopolitical dilemma is how to sustain itself as a Jewish and democratic state within secure and recognized borders. At the core of this dilemma is the balance between four components: geography (territorial depth required for security); demography (degree of national homogeneity); democracy (human rights and control of another people); and regional and international legitimacy.

The dilemma poses two primary questions: One is about how to map out borders that can create the optimal balance between the four components. Will this map imply **territorial convergence** in an effort to guarantee national homogeneity and democracy, or will it be based on **territorial dispersion** in an effort to guarantee strategic depth? The second question relates to the best way to achieve this map: Is it based on negotiations and agreement or on confrontation and rivalry?

The geopolitical problem and its underlying questions are not new. Although the geopolitical dilemma emerged in 1967 with the assumption of control of the West Bank, Golan Heights and Sinai, it has accompanied Israel from the dawn of its creation in 1948; and in some shape or form from the start of modernity, when Jews began returning to the Land of Israel.[1] What has changed dramatically in recent years is the geopolitical context underlying this dilemma. New regional developments call for original geopolitical thinking and bold policies. Alongside these developments, the following processes can be traced:

1. The collapse of the old geopolitical order, originating in the Cold War and at the center of which was the rivalry over positions and resources between the U.S. and the Soviet Union. In this old order, the Middle East was a relatively stable place, where stability was based on a balance of power between two world powers and their local allies. The fall of the Soviet Union left the U.S. as the sole superpower. However, America's invasion of Iraq and Afghanistan, its unconditional support for Israel and its ongoing economic crisis have weakened its international standing.

2. The decline of these two superpowers has left a vacuum filled by geopolitical rivalries over regional hegemony between Iran, Turkey, Egypt and Israel. The

---

[1] The subject of balance between territory, demography and regime was presented in 1936 before the British Royal Commission, known as the Peel Commission, appointed to investigate the circumstances that led to the clashes that erupted in Palestine. See Galnoor, 2009.

future relations among these regional powers are surrounded by uncertainty and may include agreements, rivalries and outright conflicts.

3. The regional developments are affected by the cultural and political transformations known as the Arab Spring. Where these transformations are heading is not yet clear. They are spawned by internal processes related to demographic changes, economic crisis, political disillusionment and global processes connected to the weakening of the nation-state, the universalization of human rights and the emergence of non-state actors and terror cells that cut across national borders. These internal processes are also generated by widespread anti-Israel sentiment, especially in Egypt and Jordan. Governments, including those that have signed peace treaties with Israel, prefer to succumb to this sentiment in order to placate the public and remain in power. These trends are likely to shape regional geopolitics in different ways.

4. The change in the nature of relations between Israel and the Palestinian Authority regarding the future solution to the Israeli-Palestinian conflict. Both sides have abandoned the negotiations option, and have turned instead to unilateral action: Israel continues to build in the territories and the Palestinians seek unilateral recognition as a state by the United Nations.

This essay, which was written in 2012, before the 2012 Gaza war and the 2013 election, is divided into four sections:

The first section examines the widespread **value-based geopolitical approaches** in Israeli society and illuminates the solutions these approaches offer to Israel's geopolitical dilemma. It can shed light on Israeli psychology, culture, fears and hopes, through the imagined geopolitical reality of various groups within Israel. The section will expose the different narratives through which various groups construct their reality, demonstrating the difficulty involved in reaching a common narrative and a policy acceptable to all. Undoubtedly, the Israeli public's worldview and values have a certain impact on the solution of Israel's dilemma. Nevertheless, the realization of any set of preferences is highly dependent upon the exercise of power, as manifested by the activities of different political actors located at different geographic levels.

The second section examines the **forces that may shape the solution to Israel's geopolitical dilemma.** This section moves beyond preferences and values and proceeds to examine the actors and processes that might affect the map of Israel's borders.

The third section is a journey into the world of **scenarios**. This part identifies possible geopolitical trends, their underlying factors and the relations between them. It detects the driving forces, the uncertainty they entail and the various possible geopolitical futures. In this way, a wide range of possible solutions to Israel's geopolitical dilemma are considered.

The fourth and final section draws some conclusions from the foregoing sections and puts forward recommendations concerning Israel's **geopolitical dilemma**.

Geopolitical Approaches: A Journey into Israel's Imaginary World

Different groups within Israeli society have developed different geopolitical approaches in an attempt to resolve its geopolitical dilemma. These approaches reflect various norms and values regarding the proper balance between geography (depth of security), demography (national identity), democracy (control of another people and human rights) and international legitimacy.[2] These values form the basis for different readings of the processes taking place in the Middle East and lead to different border maps and to different solutions to Israel's geopolitical dilemma.

The approaches prevalent among Israelis are:

1. The 1967 borders with agreed upon land swaps. This solution envisions two sovereign states for two peoples separated by borders corresponding to the armistice lines reached with Jordan at the end of Israel's War of Independence and demarcated from 1949 to 1951, with agreed-upon land swaps. The 1967 lines essentially match the 1949 lines

2. Defensible borders, comprising two border systems, namely – a security border along the Jordan Valley and a political border.

3. Interim borders involving a unilateral withdrawal by Israel from parts of the West Bank.

4. Blurred borders, which essentially implies the downgrading of borders and the creation of a bi-national state.

5. Borders of the Greater Land of Israel, comprising one Jewish state between the Mediterranean Sea and the Jordan River.

A mirror image of these approaches can be found on the Palestinian side, from the 1967 borders framework to an Islamic state from river to sea. In between them are the options for blurred borders and the creation of a binational state, as well as interim borders through gaining unilateral recognition in the United Nations for a Palestinian state, or through an interim agreement defined as either a *tahadiya* or a *hudna*.[3]

---

[2] Arieli, 2006; Hasson, 2010.

[3] PSR, 2004; Hider, 2009; Mishal and Sela, 1999; Hilal, 2007; Scham and Abu-Irshaid, 2009.

The 1967 Borders

According to this approach, a two-state solution will solve Israel's geopolitical dilemma. This approach supports one nation-state for the Jewish people and one nation-state for the Palestinian people, with secure and recognized borders for both. Israel will retain a Jewish majority as a democratic country that does not control or limit the rights of another people. The boundaries will be based on UN Security Council Resolutions 242 and 338, according to which Israel will withdraw from the territories conquered in the Six-Day War to secure borders. The basis of the agreement will be the border as it stood between 1949-1967, with agreed upon land swaps (see Illustration 1).

Israel will annex the large settlement areas established in the West Bank and compensate the Palestinians with other territories in Israel. The precise outline of the border will be determined through negotiations between the two parties.

This solution is based on four principles:

1. The basis for an agreement is the borders that existed between 1949 and 1967 with agreed upon land swaps.
2. Two capitals in Jerusalem.
3. A Palestinian right of return will only be permitted to a Palestinian state, and not to Israel.
4. Palestine will be demilitarized.

Those in Israel who support this solution include the leftwing parties Labor and Meretz, some members of Kadima and its offshoots (HaTnuah party) and the Arab parties, with some reservations regarding the character of the country.[4]

Those who support this solution argue that Israel's continued control of the territories will not bring it security but rather only intensify resentment and propagate the continuation of conflict and threat to Israel. Israel will find it difficult to hold its ground in the face of a hostile Arab world. Demographically, the Jewish population will become a minority between the Jordan River and the Mediterranean. Diplomatically, Israel is destined to become increasingly isolated in the international arena. The radical forces in the region, chief among them Iran, will garner strength by leveraging the conflict to embolden more extreme entities.

---

[4] Detailed treatment of these principles appears in Ben Caspit's interview with Ehud Barak. See Caspit, 2010.

Illustration 1:
Israel's borders
from 1949 to 1967

The Arab Spring, which has strengthened populist sentiments and identification with the Palestinians, will only bolster hatred of Israel on the Arab street; along with it, pressure on Jordan and Egypt to annul the peace treaties will only grow.

The 1967 borders with land swaps constitute the central vision presented by U.S. President Barack Obama in his May 19, 2011 speech. According to this vision, the Palestinian state will be demilitarized and the withdrawal of Israeli forces will take place in accordance with the Palestinian security forces' capacity to thwart acts of terror, weapons smuggling and maintain secure borders. The core issues – the Palestinian refugees and Jerusalem – are to be resolved later on. According to this vision, long-lasting peace is contingent upon a two-state solution, Israel as a Jewish state and Palestine as a Palestinian state, mutual recognition and peace.[5]

This is a well-known vision, parts of which have been drafted in the past by U.S. national security advisers Zbigniew Brzezinski and Brent Scowcroft.[6] Based on what these two men and President Obama have said, this vision appears to be highly encouraging and inspiring, and will change the atmosphere of the Middle East. Such an agreement will provide the Palestinians with hope and weaken Hamas as well as local and international terror groups and their supporters. It will also moderate the tensions between Israel and the Arab world by mitigating the anti-Israel sentiment of the Arab street. In this way, it will remove one of the strongest tools extremists use against Israel. Economically, the agreement will allow expedited growth by relying on the abilities of both the Jewish and Palestinian populations. Subsequently, the two societies will transform themselves into engines of growth in the Middle East and successfully compete with Dubai and Qatar.

This kind of agreement, which was also presented as part of the 2002 Arab Peace Initiative, will enable Israel to make peace with the rest of the Arab countries; and by doing so, contribute to strengthening the moderates in the region who are participating in ongoing regime change. On the regional level, the agreement is destined to strengthen Middle East stability. It will reinforce the moderate Sunni population and weaken Iran and its emissaries in the region – Hezbollah and Hamas. It will enable the US and Europe to thwart Iran's plan for nuclear armament and may also bring about an improvement in relations with Turkey.

---

[5] The White House: Office of the Press Secretary May 19, 2011.
[6] Brzezinski and Scowcroft, 2008: 79-113.

On a geostrategic level, the agreement will contribute to the strengthening of America's position in the Middle East, which has declined due to its continued support for Israel and its invasions of Iraq and Afghanistan. This will contribute to the stability Israel needs. This vision is not devoid of risks, but its realization will guarantee Israel's security and its existence as a Jewish and democratic state. As opposed to those who claim that Israel requires geographic depth, this approach argues that Israel's security is in fact contingent upon Israeli withdrawal from territory and on demographic homogeneity. Only an agreement that is considered legitimate by both sides will provide Israel with security, and this naturally requires territorial concessions.[7]

There will of course be those on both sides who try to thwart the agreement, in which case each side will be forced to decide whether to allow these entities veto power over an opportunity that is both politically and economically vital. This is why, though not without possible dangers, it provides Israel with an excellent opportunity to advance towards a solution to the conflict, and by doing so, also contributes to the stability of the entire Middle East.

This is an optimistic vision. It sees the solution to the Israeli-Palestinian conflict as the cornerstone for a solution to the problems of the Middle East. The question is: who will actually guarantee its realization? Perhaps the Israeli-Palestinian conflict is not at the root of the revolutions and conflicts in the Middle East? In that case, Israeli withdrawal to 1967 borders may turn out to be a dangerous move for the future of the country. The documents revealed by Wikileaks clearly demonstrated that regional leaders do not believe the Israeli-Palestinian conflict is at the core of the region's conflict, but rather Iran's race to nuclear armament.[8] One leader even empathized with Israel and said that it is understandable that Israel would be reluctant to give up territory when it is under threat. Another leader expressed the urgent need to put an end to the Iranian regime. The question is whether the vision nurtured around the 1967 borders is

---

[7] The Geneva Initiative is the clearest expression of this. See its main components:
http://www.geneva-accord.org/

[8] Relating to statements by Arab leaders as quoted in Wikileaks documents, Aluf Ben writes, among other things: "The statements made by Arab leaders, which saw the Iranian threat as a top concern, called on the U.S. to attack Iran, pushed the Palestinians and their troubles by the wayside, justifying the traditional Likud party line. The Israeli Right always argued that criticism of the occupation and settlement is just an excuse, a "baseless narrative," as Netanyahu called it, and that the real problem in the Middle East stems from radical regimes that support terror and are trying to attain nuclear capabilities. The Left claimed this is the Right's excuse for expanding settlements and promoting the annexation of the West Bank."

based on a thorough analysis of the factors and processes that shape the Middle East, or is it only wishful thinking? Under such circumstances, should Israel take a risk that might threaten its existence in the long run? This problem is explored in the "defensible borders" approach.

Defensible Borders

According to this approach, coping with Israel's geopolitical dilemma necessitates geographic depth that includes control of the Jordan Valley, military deployment on mountain ranges that overlook the valley and widening the corridor that leads from Jerusalem to the Dead Sea. This approach was formulated in 1967 by Yigal Allon while serving as Israel's minister of labor. Its main consideration is to guarantee Israel's security through territorial depth. This depth is necessary for preventing a hostile Arab army from entering the West Bank and taking over the mountain ranges that control the densely populated areas along the coastal plain. Most of Israel's population and economic activity is concentrated in this area. The central principle behind this approach is guaranteeing the existence of the State of Israel from any aggression directed against it. It demands geographical depth calling for a buffer area, a warning and deterrence zone that facilitates self-defense.[9] According to the Allon Plan, the Arab population in the West Bank was supposed to be an independent entity or to be part of the Kingdom of Jordan. See Illustration 2.

Former Prime Minister Yitzhak Rabin was one of the prominent supporters of this approach. In his speech in the Knesset on October 5, 1995, he said: "We will not return to the June 4, 1967 lines… Israel's security border will be along the Jordan Valley in the broad sense of the term." In his book *A Place Among the Nations*, Benjamin Netanyahu raises a principle similar to Yigal Allon's, arguing the need for a warning and deterrence space.[10] This approach is supported by many senior politicians and military professionals, among them Yuval Steinitz, Yaakov Amidror and Giora Eiland.[11]

Those who advocate this approach believe that developments in the region underscore the significance of defensible borders. The main threat is perceived to be Iran's nuclear armament. The continuation of this process will strengthen

---

[9] Allon's approach to security as far as defensible borders was published in Foreign Affairs in 1976 without a map. See Allon, 1976.

[10] Netanyahu, 2001.

[11] See the collection of articles by the Jerusalem Center for Public Affairs, 2008: http://jcpa.org/

Illustration 2: Defensible Borders according to Allon Plan

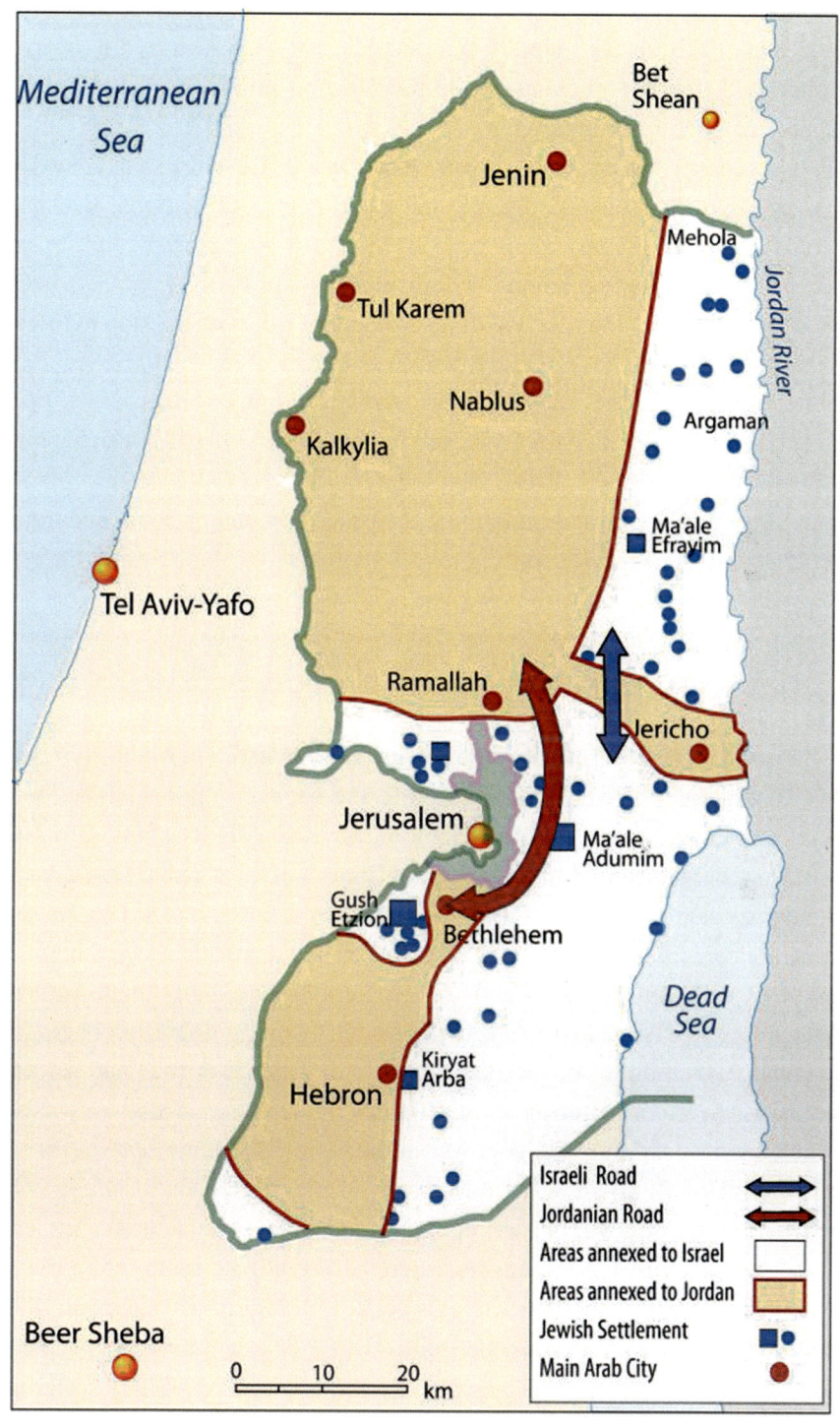

Iran and its agents in the region: Hamas and Hezbollah. This is the main threat to the Middle East - not the occupation or the settlements. The Wikileaks papers are evidence of this, as they clearly demonstrate that Arab leaders are primarily concerned with Iran's armament, while the regional importance of the Israeli-Palestinian conflict is secondary.[12]

The processes taking place in the Arab world are worrisome: Egypt is undergoing a political change that bolster the Muslim Brotherhood, which has good relations with Hamas. Their growing political power might further chill the already cold peace agreement with Israel, and possibly even dissolve it. Egypt is not stable and the absence of a strong authority may presage the rise of terrorist entities, which have already manifested themselves in attacks on Egypt and Israel from the Sinai Peninsula. Other warning signals were provided by the attack on the Israeli Embassy in Cairo and by the growing ties between Egyptian authorities and the Hamas. These developments may complicate the relations between Israel and Egypt and undermine the peace agreement. Syria and Yemen are experiencing civil war. According to this approach, the Arab Spring may turn into the Arab Winter, filled with crises and regional instability.

Relations with Turkey are tense: The strategic alliance has collapsed, the Israeli ambassador was expelled, and the Turkish prime minister has demonstrated significant hostility towards Israel.

This point of view furthermore asserts that the Palestinian Authority refuses to conduct negotiations with Israel and prefers to engage in unilateral actions in an effort to achieve international recognition as a state. This refusal is nothing new. In 2000, the Palestinians rejected Ehud Barak's offer at Camp David, and in 2008, they rejected Ehud Olmert's proposal. This rejection is a recurring strategic pattern employed by the Palestinians. The approach that argues an agreement can be reached with them is thus groundless. Furthermore, the Palestinian Authority refuses to recognize Israel as the state of the Jewish people and seeks reconciliation with Hamas, which does not recognize the State of Israel or the Oslo Accords, and continues to advocate terror.

The U.S. has lost much of its power in the region due, *inter alia*, to the way in which it treated its ally, President Mubarak. Under these circumstances, those who advocate the defensible borders approach claim that Israel must act prudently and firmly against threats and dangers. There is certainly no room for signing an agreement based on the 1967 borders. It is better to act cautiously and wait till the

---

[12] Benn, 2010.

18

situation becomes clearer. Meanwhile, the Jewish presence must be augmented in strategically important areas where it will remain in any future agreement. For this reason, the separation barrier must be completed and the territory between the security border and the political border must be seen as an unstable frontier. The only proper borders for the foreseeable future are defensible ones. This approach will provide the State of Israel with security through geographic depth.

The realities constructed by these two approaches – the 1967 borders on the one hand and defensible borders on the other – are based on highly divergent worldviews that are rooted in fundamentally disparate ideologies: Trust as opposed to mistrust, hope as opposed to suspicion, idealism as opposed to realism. Reality is interpreted by the two approaches through two completely different worldviews. While they both connect the local conflict to the broader political climate in the Middle East, they present two opposing geopolitical analyses. One looks from within the Israeli-Palestinian conflict outwards, and says that the primary players are the governments of Israel and Palestine, public opinion and peace spoilers. The second looks from outside in – within the context of the entire Middle East – towards the Israeli-Palestinian conflict. It presents Middle East politics as the primary factor in determining the behavior of both Israeli and Palestinian governments, as well as the outline of the border.

These readings produce two strategies that are both complementary and contradictory. One recommends putting an end to the Israeli-Palestinian conflict and thus furthering stability throughout the Middle East, while the other says that in order to end the conflict between Israel and Palestinians, the Middle East must first be stable.

Interim Borders

A third solution to Israel's geopolitical dilemma is the interim borders approach. According to this, Israel must be concerned, first and foremost, with its existence as a democratic state and the national homeland of the Jewish people. Continuation of the status quo, and with it, continued control of the territories, undermines the realization of these goals and constitutes a strategic threat to the state.

Without withdrawing from the territories, the demography between the Jordan River and the Mediterranean is destined to change, to the detriment of Israelis. A Jewish nation-state in which Jews are the minority, will be undemocratic. A democratic state will not be Jewish since Palestinians will ultimately become the majority. This is why the existential necessity of maintaining a Jewish nation-state requires withdrawal from the territories. Those who advocate the interim borders approach believe that continued Israeli presence in the territories would exacerbate the conflict with the Palestinians and increase Israel's diplomatic isolation. Nonetheless, at present, Israel has no partner in negotiations, and that is why Israel must take unilateral steps to disengage from the Palestinians.

Those advocating this approach diverge from both leftist and rightist arguments in Israel. The left believes withdrawal from the territories will bring about peace, the right believes Israel must remain in the territories as long as there is a conflict, whereas those who advocate this approach argue that Israel must withdraw from the territories even if the conflict continues. Israel should unilaterally withdraw to interim borders, and when conditions become ripe, it can conduct negotiations on permanent borders. The interim borders can be the borders of the separation barrier with additions of territory beyond the barrier. See Illustration 3.

This approach has received theoretical support from academics such as professors Shlomo Avineri, Dan Schueftan and Arnon Soffer.[13] Former Prime Minister Ariel Sharon set the precedent for unilateral disengagement and his successor, Ehud Olmert, advocated additional disengagement, and even raised the idea during the Second Lebanon War in 2006, although he did not ultimately try to implement it.

Those who advocate this approach can find justification for unilateral action in the steps taken by the Palestinians at the beginning of 2011.[14] Palestinians abandoned the path of negotiations and turned directly and unilaterally to the United Nations Security Council, seeking recognition as an independent state. Those advocating for interim borders see nothing wrong with this. On the contrary, international recognition of Palestine as a state means the *de facto* creation of a Palestinian state with interim borders. This will set the precedent for the establishment of a Palestinian state without permanent borders, without a solution to the refugee problem and without dividing Jerusalem. The conflict will lose its importance in the international community insofar as it is transformed from a deep national conflict to a technical conflict over borders. Furthermore, Palestinian unilateral action provides legitimacy for Israel to determine unilaterally interim borders. This is a situation in which both sides operate unilaterally and thereby advance an interim solution.

---

[13] On this subject, see: Soffer and Pollack, 2003; Schueftan, 1999; Avineri, 2008.

[14] On 29 November 2012, the United Nations General Assembly granted the Palestinian Authority the status of a nonmember observer state.

Illustration 3: Interim Borders – Route of the Security Barrier based on Israeli Government Decision of February 20, 2005

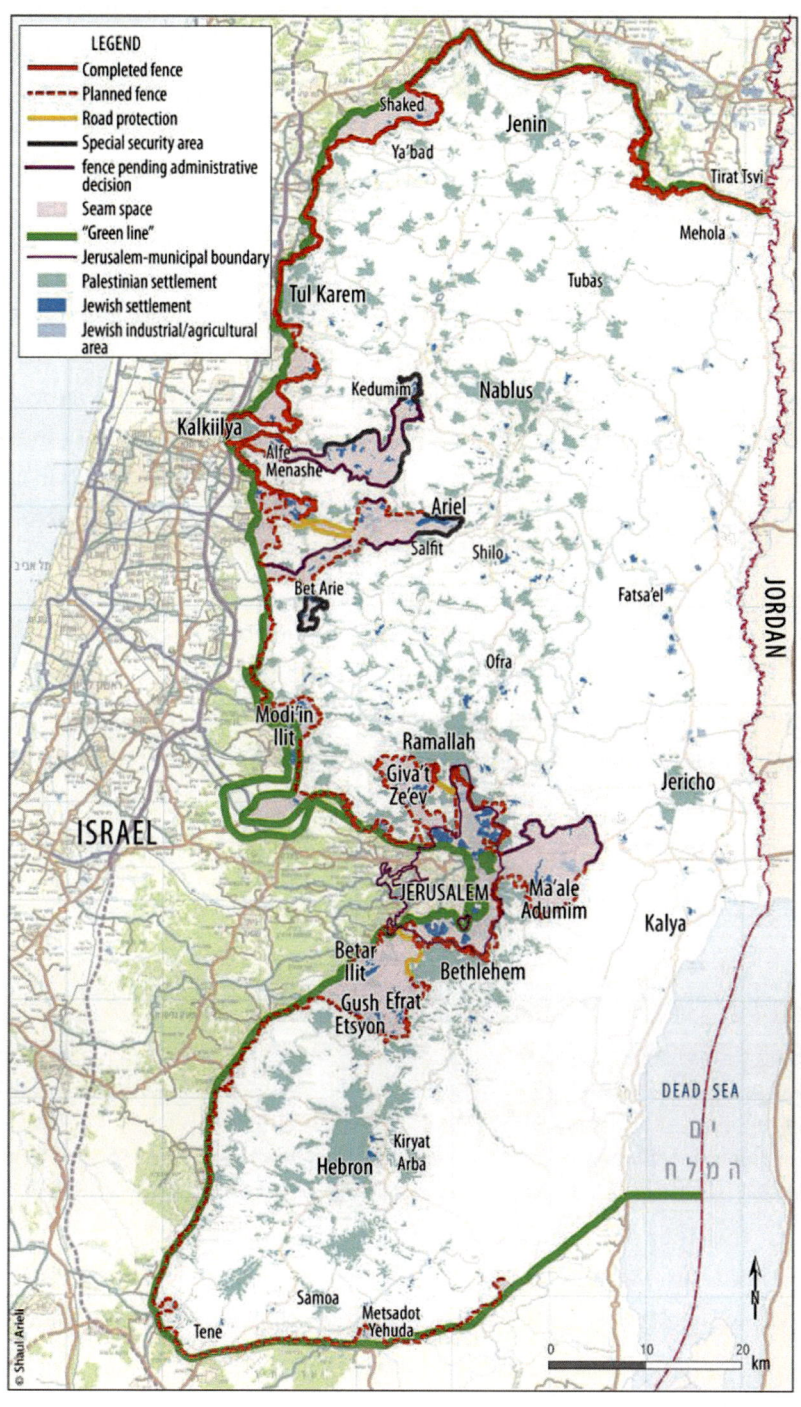

In terms of regional developments, this is the best time for a solution based on interim borders. Arab countries are busy with their own internal affairs. Egypt and Syria have weakened. Turkey's rapprochement foreign policy towards Iran's has failed. Within this context, the world may be inclined to support any Israeli withdrawal – even if only partial – from the territories.

Blurring the Lines: A Bi-national State

A fourth solution to Israel's geopolitical dilemma is through blurring the border lines. According to this approach, the Israeli-Palestinian conflict is a complex and unsolvable ethno-national conflict that has lasted for over one hundred years. Practically, Jewish settlement in the West Bank has created an irreversible situation in which two systems of settlement – Jewish and Palestinian – are irrevocably interconnected. Changing the situation through disengagement and withdrawal to other borders is impossible. No government in Israel will be able to evacuate half a million Jewish settlers dispersed throughout neighborhoods of Jerusalem and the dozens of settlements beyond the Green Line, such as Beitar Ilit, Ma'ale Adumim and Ariel. The inevitable result is a bi-national state. See Illustration 4.

Unlike the conflict with the other Arab countries, the conflict with the Palestinians is not a territorial one about borders. At the center of this conflict are historical values and symbols on which neither side is willing to compromise. For the Palestinians, the starting point is not the 1949 borders, but rather the reality in the region before 1948. According to the Palestinians and their supporters in and outside Israel, Jewish settlement was from its genesis a colonial initiative, whether it took place after 1967 or before 1948.

For Israelis, and especially the nationalist camp that includes the national-religious, national-secular and those who emigrated from the former Soviet Union with a nationalist worldview, the entire Land of Israel belongs to the Jews. This worldview opposes the notion of returning to 1967 borders. According to Yehouda Shenhav, those in favor of an agreement along the 1967 borders are living a fantasy. They are disregarding Palestinian aspirations as well as those of the settlers and their supporters. It is as if they want to return to a golden age that once existed, in which reality was shaped by a friendly group of "old style socialists" that does not exist anymore.[15]

According to Meron Benvenisti, the situation has created a *de facto* bi-national state. This reality is the product of a deadlock in talks between Israelis and

---

[15] Shenhav, 2010.

Illustration 4: Blurred Borders

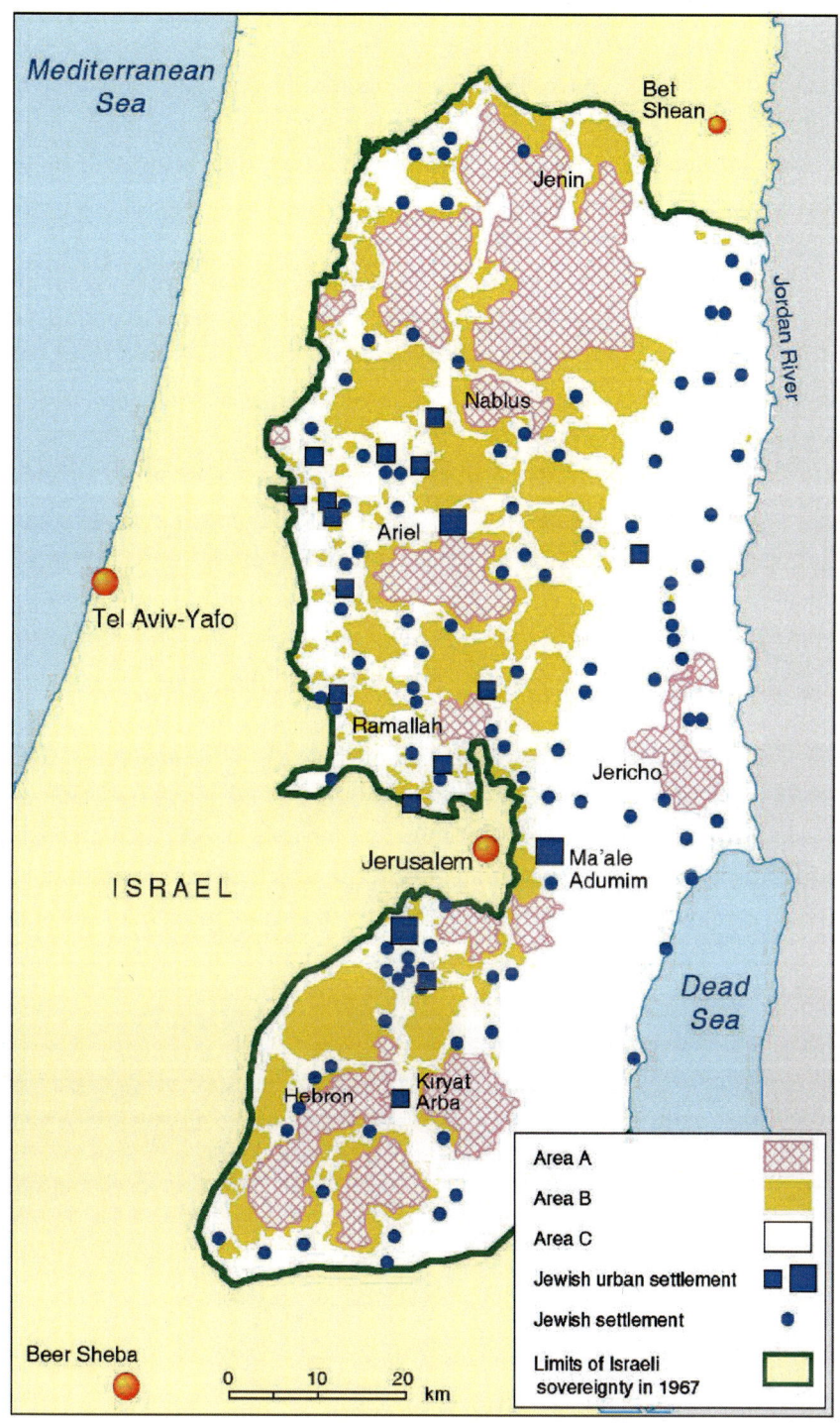

Mediterranean Sea

Bet Shean

Jenin

Jordan River

Nablus

Ariel

Tel Aviv-Yafo

Ramallah

Jericho

Jerusalem

Ma'ale Adumim

ISRAEL

Dead Sea

Kiryat Arba

Hebron

Beer Sheba

Area A

Area B

Area C

Jewish urban settlement

Jewish settlement

Limits of Israeli sovereignty in 1967

0   10   20   km

Palestinians. According to Benvenisti, Israel has created a situation in which the Palestinians have no option of developing a country with any territorial contiguity.[16] The Israeli regime in the West Bank can be characterized as apartheid or at least an ethnocracy, which privileges the ruling ethno-national group.[17] However, over time, demographic changes are bound to take place that will ultimately reshape the regime, leading it in a more democratic direction. The result will be a bi-national democratic country between the Jordan River and the Mediterranean Sea that replaces the Jewish nation-state.

Gradually, more and more Palestinians and certain Israeli groups are becoming aware that a bi-national state is inevitable. The concept of a bi-national state has accompanied the Jewish public in Israel for nearly a hundred years. Before the state was founded, Brit Shalom raised the idea, and later on Hashomer Hatzair and the Poale Zion Party.[18]

Since 1967, this idea has been held by a minority group of post-Zionists and by a few Arab-Israeli nationalists. The interesting development in recent years is that certain groups on the Israeli right have joined this circle, among them some prominent members of the Likud and the settler movement. These circles agree that Arab residents of the territories must be granted citizenship and that the entire West Bank should be annexed to Israel.[19] This is an interesting intersection of positions that reflects a conceptual convergence between two groups that are on opposite sides of the political map: post-nationalists and ultra-nationalists. What they share in common is the belief in the persistence of the territorial status quo. Israeli advocates of the blurred borders approach can find support for their position in the findings of the Palestinian Strategic Group, which argues that failure to be recognized as an independent state will bring about the collapse of the Palestinian Authority, the transfer of responsibility for Palestinian territory and its residents to Israel and the establishment of a bi-national state.[20]

---

[16] Benvenisti, 2010.
[17] Levy, 2011.
[18] Heller, 2000, 161-163.
[19] Arens, 2010.
[20] See the proposal made by Palestine Strategy Group, 2011.

Borders of the Greater Land of Israel

The fifth and last solution to Israel's geopolitical dilemma is expansion to the borders of the Greater Land of Israel. According to this solution, Jewish settlement must spread out across the entire Land of Israel for both religious and security reasons. The border should be at the Jordan River and the Palestinian Authority should be disbanded. Arabs living in Judea and Samaria should be treated in one of three ways: Israeli annexation of the territories and granting its residents citizenship; granting local autonomy to Palestinian enclaves in the area; or "transfer." The most popular approach at present among those who advocate this approach is the cantonal approach delineated by Avigdor Lieberman. According to this, Palestinians will enjoy autonomy in the enclaves surrounded by Jewish settlements. They will vote in Jordanian elections (See Illustration 5). Critics of this approach argue that this is a surefire recipe for an apartheid state.

Recent developments in the Middle East strengthen advocates of this approach. Its supporters assert that the Palestinians have proven that they will never recognize Israel's right to exist as the national homeland of the Jewish people. They rather prefer to appeal to the UN and achieve international recognition without negotiating with Israel. This is clear testimony of the fact they are unwilling to recognize the right of the Jewish people to a nation-state. In due course, they seek to destroy the State of Israel from without by attaining international support and through hostile forces from within.

This activity is supported by the Arab world and a large bloc of countries that are either hostile or that fail to understand the Palestinian deceit. In light of these processes, Israel must remain in the volatile space known as the West Bank, which is no other than Judea and Samaria, the cradle of Jewish civilization. This region is characterized by the absence of law, police and a court system. Leaving this area may pose a real threat to the State of Israel. Changes in the Arab world are bound to strengthen the extremists, and the option that a hostile army will enter the vacated space and attack Israel should not be ruled out. Those who evacuated Gush Katif endured rocket barrages in Beer Sheba and Ashkelon. Those who evacuate Judea and Samaria will endure rockets in Tel Aviv and Jerusalem.

The concept of the Greater Land of Israel is not new. It has existed since the dawn of Zionism. The fathers of Zionism, Theodor Herzl and Ze'ev Jabotinsky, drew maps that sometimes even spread beyond the borders of the Greater Land of Israel.[21] The map submitted by the Zionist mission to the Peace Conference in

---

[21] Herzl, (1902) 1960; Jabotinsky, (1937) 1948.

**Illustration 5:
Borders of
the Greater
Land of Israel**

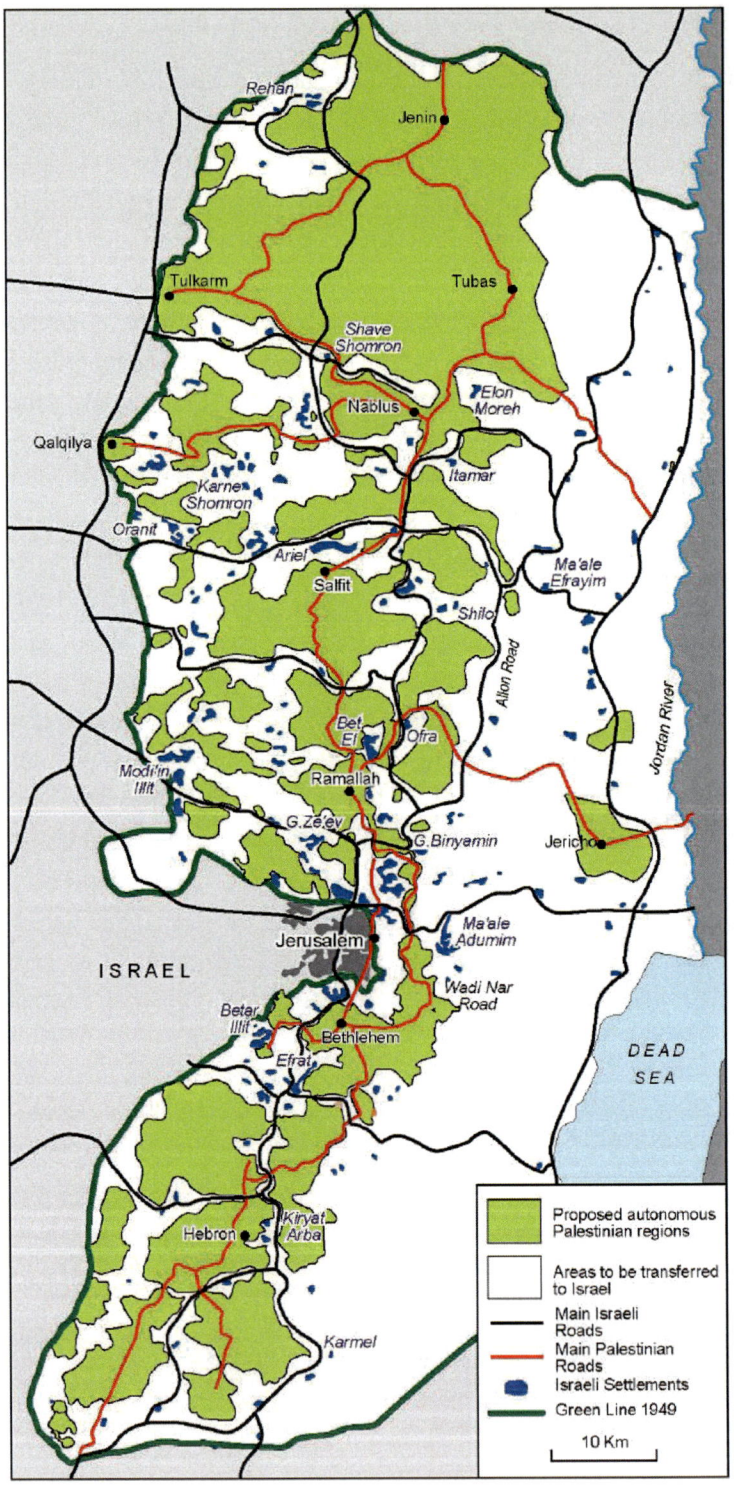

Rehan

Jenin

Tulkarm

Tubas

Shave
Shomron

Elon
Moreh

Nablus

Qalqilya

Itamar

Karne
Shomron

Oranit

Ariel

Ma'ale
Efrayim

Salfit

Shilo

Allon Road

Jordan River

Bet
El

Ofra

Modi'in,
Illit

Ramallah

G.Ze'ev

G.Binyamin

Jericho

ISRAEL

Jerusalem

Ma'ale
Adumim

Betar
Illit

Wadi Nar
Road

Bethlehem

Efrat

DEAD
SEA

Kiryat
Arba

Hebron

Karmel

Proposed autonomous
Palestinian regions

Areas to be transferred
to Israel

Main Israeli
Roads

Main Palestinian
Roads

Israeli Settlements

Green Line 1949

10 Km

1919 presented extended borders. However, over the years Zionist leaders came to the practical realization that Zionism was not created in order to turn Palestine into a Jewish state but rather in order to create a Jewish state in Palestine. The recognition of the existence of another people in the region led to the idea of partition.

Since the Likud Party assumed power in 1977 and Ariel Sharon was appointed to head the Ministerial Committee on Settlement Affairs, the power of those who advocate settlement throughout the Land of Israel has increased. The signing of the Oslo Accords has not changed the situation and in the period since, the Jewish population in the territories has tripled. The current Israeli government's refusal to freeze settlement construction is clear evidence for the fact that the Greater Land of Israel approach is alive and kicking among the country's leaders, albeit surreptitiously. Those who openly support it and insist on remaining in all parts of the historic Land of Israel are the national religious parties of "Habayit Hayehudi" (The Jewish Home) and "Haichud Haleumi" (The National Union).

Solutions to the Geopolitical Dilemma – A Comparative Perspective

These five approaches present four different solutions to the geopolitical dilemma. The 1967 borders approach suggests a resolution of the conflict through negotiations and economic cooperation, following a withdrawal to permanent borders. The defensible borders and interim borders approaches suggest a solution based upon conflict management. The blurred borders approach suggests a transformation of the conflict – from a territorial conflict to a conflict about the character of a bi-national state, its political institutions and shared spaces. The Greater Land of Israel approach suggests the elimination of the conflict through annexation, restrictions and population transfer. Politically speaking, these solutions can be grouped into two major categories: conflict and agreement oriented policies.

Beside the political differences, two different territorial options can be discerned. One option is territorial convergence, based upon withdrawal to borders of some sort, whether permanent or temporary. This option allows for the redrawing of borders to take place in stages, at first to defensible or interim borders and then to permanent agreed upon borders. The second option is territorial expansion, whereby the land between the Jordan River and the Mediterranean Sea becomes one political entity. Both nationalists and post-nationalists advocate this approach and support a blurring of the borders. Both believe that the political regime that takes over will serve its goals: a national or a post-national state.

Advocates of the different approaches are convinced that they have an accurate reading of the history and understand which way it is heading. On the basis of what they see as a rational and objective understanding of history, they think they can explain why their solution to Israel's geopolitical problem is the appropriate and inevitable one. Conflict resolution by returning to the 1967 borders is unavoidable due to notions of morality and progress; the world is no longer willing to accept colonialism, believes in freedom and human rights and sees the continuation of the occupation as anachronistic and unacceptable, both politically and ethically. The defensible borders approach is unavoidable because of the imperative of national security. The world is a chaotic and unpredictable place – without power and strategic depth Israel may disappear from the map. The solution of interim borders is inevitable due to the national demographic threat. If Israel does not withdraw to interim borders even without an agreement, it will cease to exist as a Jewish nation-state with a democratic character. The blurred borders solution is unavoidable due to the historic and geographical complexity both communities live in. Under such circumstances, there is no chance for a solution based on territorial division and remapping of borders. The Greater Land of Israel solution is inevitable for reasons of security, heritage, history and divine promise.

Such approaches can easily drift into naïve realism. Each group is convinced it understands the situation better than anyone else and that its solution is the most appropriate. The result is inability to conduct a dialogue that cuts across political boundaries and disregard of other forces that may shape the solution to Israel's geopolitical dilemma. Against this backdrop, intense conflicts and struggles may arise between different groups within Israeli society at the roots of which are divergent cultural codes. The reading of reality is characterized by a lack of openness and awareness of other forces and the possibility that those forces may behave in different ways in certain situations. The tendency characterizing naïve realism is to force one single interpretation of reality that is considered appropriate and correct.

THE DRIVING FORCES

Ideology and values play a substantial role in the shaping of history and the various values and interests that guide different geopolitical readings are of great importance. However, there are other forces operating alongside them that deserve attention as well. Studies conducted in the field identify a number of forces at work on local, regional and global levels. These forces ultimately determine which solution of those reviewed above will eventually be realized.

On the local level, the driving forces are governments, leadership, coalitions, social elites that shape public opinion, civil society, which includes organizations and groups that support or oppose the peace process, and public opinion itself. From among these factors, leadership plays a very important role. It must take into account the regional developments, consider internal preferences and create a balance between the two. It must also reach decisions and implement them. Without the ability to lead, facts on the ground may be determined by extreme forces that oppose any agreement and are trying to sabotage it.

The most important factors that for a long time have shaped the Israeli-Palestinian conflict include the government of Israel, the Palestinian Authority and the Hamas government in Gaza. The Arab Spring substantially heightened the importance of civil society and demonstrated that it has the power to overthrow authoritarian regimes. However, the overthrow of such regimes is only a first stage in what might be a long transformation. It is by no means clear what kind of regime will be eventually formed and to what degree it will be a moderate and democratic regime that can help advance a solution to the conflict. The political ascendance of the Islamic movements in Tunisia and Egypt casts a long shadow over the option of democratic regimes taking form in those countries.

On a regional level, the Middle East is undergoing some substantial changes. Old alliances, like the one between Turkey and Israel, are falling apart, and the alliance between Iran and Syria seems to be on shaky ground. Different countries in the Middle East seek to enhance their strategic weight through military arms races and by diplomatic and economic means. In this context, it is important to pay attention to Turkey and the coalition it seeks to establish through the isolation of Israel, as well as the coalition being formed between Iran and Iraq. Egypt is becoming a secondary power due to the political and economic crisis there. Rivalries between Sunnis and Shi'ites in the region are sharpening, as is evident from what is happening in Syria and Bahrain, for example. Islamic power is growing in the region and the question is whether a regional Islamic or Arab coalition will be formed and how that will influence Israel's positions regarding its borders.

On a global level, the decline of Russian and U.S. power is salient. These two superpowers used to play an important role in the stabilization of the Middle East but their waning has created a vacuum in the area that could be filled by new superpowers such as India and China. Russia aspires to strengthen its standing in the region, while the U.S. continues to support Israel, which has damaged its own position. The U.S. and other members of the Quartet – the European Union, Russia and the United Nations – are involved in aiding the Palestinian Authority and the U.S. is still trying to mediate between the two sides. Alongside these forces are processes of globalization, which bring new ideas and technologies to the region.

These historical developments are characterized by a high level of uncertainty regarding the impact of the driving forces on Israel's geopolitical map. For a long time the driving forces at the local level played a leading role in this regard. The 1948 war, the Six-Day war, the Oslo Accords, the peace treaties with Egypt and Jordan, the withdrawal from Sinai and the construction of the separation barrier were all initiated by local leadership or the product of bilateral initiatives.

Today it seems as though the period in which local driving forces predominantly shape the geopolitical reality has run its course. The pendulum has been swinging from the local to the regional and global levels. This is largely due to the weakening of local leaders on the one hand, and the sharpening of rivalries between superpowers and other countries in the region on the other.

The collapse of the old geopolitical order in the Middle East, at the center of which was the balance of power between the Soviet Union, the U.S. and their allies, has opened the door to new regional players. Iran's race to reach nuclear capability, the rise of Turkey and the rivalry between Sunnis and Shi'ites all intensify the impact of such regional developments. The political changes in North African countries and some Middle Eastern states indicate the likelihood of a long transitional period whose end result is unclear. Under such circumstances, it is difficult to imagine that the local leadership in Israel and the Palestinian Authority will make far-reaching decisions that lead to an agreement. It seems more reasonable that they will be heavily influenced by actions undertaken by the superpowers, regional forces and internal processes occurring in the Arab world. This means that confronting Israel's geopolitical dilemma will require preparation for processes that go beyond the local level, and which demand new strategic thinking equipped to deal simultaneously with global and regional developments.

The Global Level

In the past, the Middle East functioned as a shatter belt.[22] Although it was characterized by divisions and rivalries and multiple wars, its instability was contained throughout the Cold War by the two superpowers. The invasion of Sinai during the Israel's War of Independence or during the 1956 Suez Crisis ended due to an American ultimatum.

This era came to an end due to the decline of Russia's power and more recently, the decline of U.S. power. By no means, however, have these powers withdrawn from the region. The U.S. has significant financial and strategic interests in the area, and Russia has been trying to restore its geopolitical standing. At the same time, the European Union and China have increased their involvement. While the EU is trying to act as a stabilizing force, Russia is trying to restore its geopolitical sphere of influence and China is still in a waiting position, as it attempts to attain the regional resources necessary for its economic growth. Illustration 6 demonstrates the central global forces fighting for geostrategic positions and economic resources the region.

Illustration 6: Global forces and geostrategic and economic rivalries

USA — China

Superpowers
The New Great Game

Geostrategic competition
over resources and positions

EU — Russia

---

[22] "A region torn by internal conflicts whose fragmentation increased by the intervention of external major powers seeking to extend their influence over the region." See Cohen, 2009, 5.

The United States

The fall of the Soviet empire in 1989 opened a new chapter in the region's history. For a short period it seemed as if a new world order had emerged: A world led solely by the United States, in which the "end of history" was indeed imminent. American success in the First Gulf War (1991), when it astutely created a broad coalition that included Arab countries, determined this new world order for a period. However, America's involvement in Afghanistan and in Iraq in the Second Gulf War (2003) proved that the new order created was fragile and temporary. Current processes in the Middle East indicate a decline in American power.

Several factors have contributed to this decline: Arab resentment towards the U.S. as a result of its involvement in Iraq and ongoing support for Israel; the breakdown of the strategic alliance between Turkey and Israel that enabled the U.S. to rely on a supportive axis; regime change in Egypt, which in recent years was a strong U.S. ally. The withdrawal of American forces from Iraq may spawn a connection between Iran and powerful Shi'ites controlling Iraq, paving the way for Iran to become a dominant power in the region.[23] Finally, the American failure to win the war in Afghanistan and the conflict with Pakistan may further weaken its position in the region.

Obama's policy of reconciliation with the Muslim and Arab world did not achieve the anticipated results. The American abandonment of Egyptian President Hosni Mubarak was interpreted by monarchies and autocratic rulers in the region as clear evidence that the U.S. cannot be relied on in times of crisis. The democratic forces that blossomed during the Arab Spring did not generate any dividends for the U.S., as the Arab public continues to maintain its reservations. America's popularity and capability to influence the situation in Egypt is low. The rise to power of Islamic parties in Tunisia and Egypt may hurt America's ties to countries in the region in the long run. The U.S. has also lost its ability to influence the Palestinian Authority, which became clear when it was unable to thwart the Palestinian appeal for unilateral recognition at the UN at the end of 2011. Its ability to influence Israel has also proven weak, as evident from the issue surrounding a settlement freeze.

The diminishment of American power also stems from deeper processes rooted in the political and economic crisis the country is going through. This is most evident in the high rate of unemployment, an unprecedented budget deficit and the inability to formulate a long-term economic plan approved by both the

---

[23] Eizenstadt. S.E. 2011.

Executive and Congress. Under these circumstances, it is unlikely to expect the U.S. to have another wide-ranging involvement in other Middle Eastern countries. American withdrawal from Iraq and Afghanistan and the stated policy of Secretary of State Hillary Clinton to shift the diplomatic, economic and military center of gravity to Southeast Asia signals a waning interest in the Middle East.[24] These developments are augmented by the three deficiencies in U.S. policy: an absence of resource allocation for maintaining control in the region, an absence of ideological commitment, and an absence of leadership.[25]

The result is an adaptive and ineffective policy that fails to anticipate future developments. As America declines, global demographic and economic power is in the process of moving from the West to the East. India and China are emerging as new financial powers partly responsible for the fact that the global economic crisis is not even worse.

Within this global framework, a special relationship has been forged since the Six-Day War between the U.S. and Israel, characterized by trust and economic, security and political cooperation. This relationship is based not only on common strategic interests – such as blocking (formerly) the Soviet Union and (now) Russia and its allies in the Arab world, but also on common values. The narrative that developed has praised the similarity between the two countries in terms of their historical evolvement and their future goals. These similarities were based on pioneering settlement in wild and hostile territory; struggling with difficult terrain and a hostile population; and building a modern, democratic and advanced society. Both societies strongly feel they have been imparted with a unique mission.[26] The happiness expressed on the Arab street following the September 11 terror attacks led to a strengthening of the ties between the two societies and bolstered American support for Israel. Finally, an American Jewish population that is deeply involved in U.S. politics plays an important role in the strengthening of relations between the US and Israel.

The Obama Presidency has been characterized by a complex relationship with Israel: continued support of Israeli security, including an understanding of Israeli nuclear policy; anti-terror operations; refusal to recognize Hamas rule in

---

[24] Clinton, November 2011.

[25] Ferguson, 2004.

[26] On the special relationship, see Obama's address to the Israeli Presidential Conference, in which he said the alliance between the two countries is far more than strategic, as it is based on faith shared by Israel and the U.S. in the ability of democratic countries to change the future: http://www.tog.co.il/he/New.aspx?id=2101 (Hebrew)

Gaza; and encouragement of the Palestinian Authority to recognize Israel as the national homeland of the Jewish people.[27] At the same time, there are disputes that cannot be ignored. The American administration has over the years consistently supported the establishment of a Palestinian state alongside Israel and has repeatedly denounced building of settlements in the West Bank. In this sense, Obama's presidency is no different than previous ones. He and the secretary of state have offered Prime Minister Netanyahu generous compensation for a temporary settlement freeze, but the Israeli prime minister refused.

The roots of the dispute are even more profound. The American government believes the solution to the Israeli-Palestinian conflict, once achieved, could serve as the cornerstone of geopolitical transformation in the Middle East. It will generate hope in the Palestinian Authority and strengthen moderate countries in the Middle East, and as a result, enable the isolation of Iran and the terrorist groups it supports. According to the U.S. administration, these developments may well serve Israel's interests.[28] Moreover, a settlement between Israel and the Palestinian Authority will diminish resentment towards the U.S. and improve its standing in the Middle East. On the other hand, the Israeli government believes that a failure to stop Iran's nuclear program will diminish the prospects for peace and undermine American influence in the Middle East. This dispute has pushed the Israeli-Palestinian conflict further down on the American agenda, which seems to be an expression of despair and of taking a step back from the issue.

It is against this backdrop that relations between the Israeli prime minister and the U.S. president and secretary of state have reached their low point. The tensions thawed a bit during the presidential campaign and Obama's increasing need of Jewish support. Nonetheless, the dispute between Israel and the U.S. on the Palestinian issue has become even more conspicuous these days, and the question of whether Israel is an asset or a liability continues to be raised.

Israel, which has in the past relied on western support, will have to adapt to these international changes and establish a new global network of relationships.[29] It will also have to closely monitor the geopolitical policy of its friend and ally, the U.S., in order to see how much it is willing to invest in the Middle East, while also dealing with new challenges in Southeast Asia and the Pacific Ocean. Long term demographic changes in the U.S. should also be cautiously observed, especially the rise of the Hispanic population, whose commitment to the shared

---

[27] Makovsky, 2010.

[28] See Obama's vision as it was expressed in his speech from May 19, 2011.

[29] Eizenstadt, 2011.

values of Israel and the U.S. may be lower. Israel must pay attention to the broader strategic context: Does the U.S. still support a special alliance with Israel the way it did after the fall of the Soviet Union? Does this alliance serve or harm Israel's confrontation with Iran? Is it not in the interest of the U.S. to strengthen its ties to Iran and Turkey even if that damages relations with Israel?

In an era of national and regional upheavals in the Middle East, it is necessary to attribute great importance to the role of geopolitical interests and not rely solely on the shared values evident in a special relationship. No one can guarantee that the special relationship of yesterday will not be replaced by the concrete, objective interests of tomorrow.

Resurgent Russia

Russia's economic crisis and the parliamentary democracy that characterized Boris Yeltsin's presidency ended with Vladimir Putin's rise to power in 2000. Yeltsin's era has been replaced with political centralism, economic recovery – based upon energy resources – and increasing friction with the West as Russia seeks to reestablish its geopolitical spheres of influence in Europe, Central Asia and the Middle East.[30] The Putin-Medvedev regime's geopolitics is characterized by two central components: A national component of pragmatic defense of borders and state security, and a global and regional component focused on positioning Russia as the dominant civilization in Eurasia, which balances and mediates between Christianity and Islam. The global and regional components, which are based on Russia's geostrategic positioning, its military strength and its cultural-ideological worldviews, are geared towards undermining the unipolar notion in global geopolitics and replacing it with a multipolar notion, while creating a new world order. The practical expression of this idea is the attempt to restore Russia's influence and control in areas that were once part of the Soviet Empire.[31]

Russian geopolitics is naturally predisposed to clashes with the West and especially the United States. This clash is particularly evident in Russia's adamant objection to the expansion of the North Atlantic Treaty Organization (NATO) to include countries considered to be its backyard: Ukraine to the west and Georgia to the south. Fierce competition between the U.S. and Russia has been also registered in central Asian republics formerly part of the Soviet Union.

---

[30] See Yitzhak Brodny's lecture on the subject: "Russian politics in a new era."
(Hebrew: http://www.youtube.com/watch?v=2UrNMuSy48U)
[31] Morozova, 2009.

In the Middle East, friction with the West derives from Russia's support for the radical axis led by Iran, support for Syria despite its regime's brutal oppression of citizens and support for Hamas, classified by the U.S. as a terror organization.[32]

Obama's "reset" policy was meant to diminish the geopolitical conflict by making certain concessions to Russia, including foregoing its stationing of anti-ballistic missiles in Europe, signing off on reducing strategic arms, recognizing Russia's special position in the former Soviet republics and abandoning the expansion of NATO in these areas; as well as Russia's integration in international operations together with Western countries and specifically the peace process in the Middle East and its cooperation with NATO projects. Russia has, in exchange, been requested to join the sanctions against Iran and cooperate with the U.S. and NATO against radical Islamic entities.[33]

These developments attest to conflicting trends in Russian geopolitics. On the one hand, Russia partially participates in applying sanctions against Iran and is examining options of allying more closely with the European Union and NATO. On the other hand, it seeks to form an alliance with Iran that will limit American influence in the Middle East. The link to Iran does not necessarily mean a strategic alliance between the two, but rather a partnership characterized by mutual suspicion. This is due to Russia's sensitivity to the establishment of a radical Islamic axis with nuclear capabilities that would threaten its southern borders. Russia is also attentive to its international position as a country subject to international treaties, which seeks to maintain close relations with the West.[34] Under these circumstances, it appears that returning to the "cold war" is most unlikely; however regional frictions and rivalries are certainly plausible. Russia will undoubtedly look to strengthen its geopolitical influence in South Asia and the Middle East, and the 2008 war in Georgia is clear evidence of this trend.

China is another country to consider while looking at the Middle East geopolitical map. It has a significant interest in securing its energy supply from the region, and seeks to foster its relations with Iran and the Gulf States. China may cooperate with Russia in an effort to build a power that can contend with the U.S.

The ambivalent nature of Russian geopolitics is also apparent in its relations with Israel. Russia has been blocking any attempt to thwart Iranian nuclear

---

[32] See Shearman's survey, 2009.

[33] Magen Bagno-Moldavsky, 2011.

[34] Regarding the complex relationship between Russia and Iran and the limitations of the current strategic alliance, see: Aras and Ozbay, 2008.

armament and opposes condemnation of Iran in the Security Council as well as increasing economic sanctions against it. Russian contractors are assisting in the construction of the nuclear reactor in Bushehr. Russia also diplomatically and financially supports Arab countries in conflict with Israel, providing the oppressive regime in Syria with advanced weapons, some of which make their way to Hezbollah. Russia has also recognized Hamas rule in the Gaza Strip despite the fact that Israel and the U.S. treat it as a terror organization.[35] On the other hand, over a million Israeli citizens have arrived from Russia, which contributes to the strengthening of cultural relations between the two countries. Russia strategically cooperates with Israel on space research and commercial relations between the two countries have improved in recent years.

These conflicting trends raise questions about Russia's policies in general and regarding Israel in particular. Is Russia guided by an imperial Tsarist or Bolshevist geopolitical vision, or by a pragmatic one? Does Russia's regional involvement take Israeli interests into account or is it hostile to them? Have policymakers in Russia decided upon these issues, or are they still under dispute due to various players pulling in different directions? The uncertainty surrounding these questions suggests that Russia's operations in the Middle East can move in different and conflicting directions.

The European Union

The Barcelona Process, which began in 1995, marked the beginning of a process of social and economic relations between the EU and countries in North Africa and the Middle East. This process has continued with the "European Neighborhood Policy," signed between the EU and countries in the region. The EU has been operating to stabilize the region through political reforms, at the center of which is the promotion of democracy, economic development and social-cultural cooperation.[36] A 2011 EU document entitled "A New Response to a Changing Neighbourhood" emphasizes that the EU is not only seeking to improve relations with countries in the Middle East but also to forge partnerships with civil society, in an effort to strengthen democracy and promote human rights.[37] At the same time, EU states have not waived the option of military involvement in the Middle

---

[35] Epstein, 2007. Israel, Russia and the Failed Romance? Russia In Global Politics, 7 (Russian)

[36] For texts on the Barcelona process and its cooperative agreements, see: Commission of the European Communities, 2004.

[37] European Commission, 2011.

East, especially when it serves their strategic and economic interests. A clear example is France's involvement in toppling the Qaddafi regime in Libya. The EU's stabilizing presence is overshadowed by the deep economic crisis engulfing its member states.

The EU's relationship with Israel is ambivalent: Alongside declarations of strengthening ties and involvement in the peace process, the EU has blamed Israel for the impasse in solving the Israeli-Palestinian conflict. The EU has condemned Israel several times for its continued settlement construction and its policies in East Jerusalem, and has suspended the upgrade of relations with Israel. Even Germany, which has traditionally supported Israel, has begun publicly criticizing Israel's treatment of Palestinians.[38]

The EU's criticism of Israel has been intensifying, especially in western European countries, due to demographic changes. There has been a dramatic increase in the Muslim population in certain countries in recent years, especially in France and Germany. This may engender some significant political changes towards Israel. A counter-tendency is associated with the rise of right wing parties that oppose Muslim immigration. These parties, which have a long anti-Semitic tradition, may provide Israel with support, declaring that Judea and Samaria are part of the State of Israel. It is important to remember that Israel has already been let down by European countries twice before, once during the Six-Day War and then during the 1973 War. Israel thus tends to be suspicious and cautious regarding the EU and its ability to serve as a fair arbiter in the conflict.

North Atlantic Treaty Organization (NATO)

Military cooperation in the Middle East between European countries and the U.S., as is evident in NATO actions, will continue to play an important role in the region. Despite its decline, the U.S. is expected to play an important role due to its various interests in the region: energy sources, maritime routes and areas of great strategic importance, the guarantee of Israeli security and the war on terror. American power was on display in September 2011 when President Obama intervened to help save Israeli diplomatic staff in Egypt during a raid by an angry mob on the Israeli Embassy. Obama also threatened Iran regarding the closing of the Straits of Hormuz. American presence in the Middle East may taper off as a result of the rise of other regional powers that wish to increase their strategic influence in the region, but the U.S. remains a central force, nonetheless.

---

[38] Stein, 2010.

Geopolitical Implications for Israel

The chief geopolitical problem that Israel will face as it considers the map of its future borders is America's position in the area and its ability to guarantee agreements that Israel would sign. The decline of U.S. power is likely to inhibit the realization of a solution in which Israel withdraws to 1967 borders and could lead to the adoption of other geopolitical options. The prospects of an agreement based on 1967 borders may further decrease due to Russian and Chinese support of the Shi'ite axis and given the rising power of radical entities in the region. It is therefore in Israel's utmost interest to assist in strengthening American presence in the region, which can act as a guarantor of a permanent agreement between Israel and the Palestinian Authority.

Regional Level

The regional balance of power in the Middle East has been recently shattered. Gradually, a new order is being created whose effect on Israel is not yet clear. Yesterday's regional structures have faded away, and the new developments are surrounded by great uncertainty. Of the rogue countries that have threatened regional and world peace in the past – Iraq, Libya, Syria and Iran – only the latter has remained as a powerful regional power. Iraq and Libya have seen regime change and Syria is immersed in a cruel and bloody civil war. Civil wars continue to plague Yemen and Somalia; both are failed states that are incapable of guaranteeing security, financial stability and basic services to their residents.

The radical axis led by Iran, which included Syria, Hezbollah and Hamas, has suffered a serious blow, but has not yet collapsed. The moderate axis of pragmatic countries with a pro-American orientation, including Israel, Egypt, Jordan and the Gulf States, has suffered a serious crisis due to the ousting of Hosni Mubarak. Collapse of a regime friendly to the U.S. raises some serious questions about American presence in Egypt and the nature of future cooperation between the two countries. This question has been aggravated with the rise of the Muslim Brotherhood to power in Egypt's parliament and the election of Mohamed Morsi, a member of the Muslim brotherhood, as president. The question is whether such a regime would follow the reformist Islamic model similar to the one presented by Recep Tayyip Erdoğan's Justice and Development Party in Turkey or a fundamentalist Islamic line that is hostile to democracy and to the peace treaty with Israel.

Alongside these national changes, a regional geostrategic competition is developing between the radical Shi'ite-oriented forces and the Sunni-oriented axis. Proxy wars between the two axes are apparent in Syria and Yemen, and intense conflicts are evident in key places like Bahrain, where Saudi Arabia and Iran are at odds.

The strategic competition points to a clear process in which several countries wish to increase their strategic weight in the region through military, economic, cultural, religious and diplomatic means. This process could take different forms: large-scale regional war, creation of a regional balance of power or the emergence of a hegemonic power in the region. The main players in this process are Turkey, Iran and, to a lesser extent, Egypt and Israel. (See Illustration 7)

Illustration 7: Regional Powers

Iran's Goal of Regional Hegemony

Until 2003, there was a balance of power between Iraq and Iran in the Persian Gulf. The Second Gulf War in 2003 and the collapse of the regime in Iraq made Iran the dominant player in the region. With the American pullout from Iraq, Iran has become the strongest power in the Persian Gulf. With a population of 79 million, military prowess and the potential of nuclear capabilities, Iran is able to play a central role in the region and even take control of the Persian Gulf. An attack on its nuclear facilities would trigger the closing of the Straits of Hormuz, through which a fifth of the world's oil production is shipped. The closing of the Straits would raise the price of oil by 50 percent and seriously harm the global economy.[39] An attack on Iran's nuclear facilities thus necessitates a strike on its naval operations and ultimately its ground forces as well. Israel is not prepared for such an operation. The only entity that can do this is the United States, and the likelihood of it embarking on another war in the Middle East is low. It seems that the world's superpowers – which at one time were practically omnipotent – are currently incapable of constraining Iran's race to nuclear power.

President Obama's attempt to initiate dialogue with Iran regarding its nuclear armament failed and financial sanctions against Iran are not achieving their goals. There is almost nothing to stop Iran from becoming a major regional power that threatens its neighbors in the Persian Gulf and U.S. interests in the area. In addition, Iran has allies throughout the region: Hezbollah in Lebanon and to a lesser extent, Hamas and radical Islamic groups in Gaza. Iran can wage an ongoing war with Israel through these proxy entities located to the north and south of the country. And yet this analysis deserves some qualifications.

Contrary to the impression conveyed by Iran's antagonistic conduct, it is a country on the defensive.[40] The primary goal of Iran's religious leadership is to guarantee its survival and continued political control. The Sunni states surrounding Iran, such as Saudi Arabia and the Gulf countries, are hostile and suspicious. Shi'ites have always been a minority in the Muslim world, at times a persecuted minority. Iran's attempt to support the repressed Shi'ite majority in Bahrain ended with Saudi involvement, which foiled the move, and Iran's support for the Bashar al-Assad Syrian regime is countered by Sunni states that support the Syrian opposition.

The social unrest in Iran remains and despite being repressed by an iron fist, it continues to bubble up under the surface. In Iran itself there are throngs of minority communities that could rebel, including the Azeri and Kurdish populations. It is therefore no wonder that the ayatollahs' regime in Iran feels threatened and

---

[39] Ginzburg, January 29, 2012.

[40] For an intriguing analysis of Iran's position and future relations with the U.S., see Friedman, 2011. He argues that the U.S. will choose to strengthen its ties with Iran even at the cost of confronting Israel and Saudi Arabia. The precedent for the U.S. to reach out to a hostile country is F.D.R.'s alliance with the Soviet Union during WWII and Richard Nixon's ties with China during the Cold War. Such a scenario would reflect the U.S. choice to ally with the Shi'ite minority in the Middle East at the expense of its relations with the Sunni majority. In the long run, this could damage the trust in the U.S. and drive Arab counties to turn to other powers. Finally this could accelerate the nuclear armament race in the region.

is reactionary. The regime is convinced that developing nuclear capabilities is its insurance policy for survival. The West's invasion of Iraq and intervention in Libya taught Iran an important lesson: If these countries possessed nuclear weapons, it is likely these interventions would not have taken place. Condemnation of Israel and threats of its destruction should be understood within this context as rhetoric intended to enlist the support of the world's Sunni population by drawing attention to the eternal enemy, Israel. Ayatollah Ali Khamenei's speech, in which he described Israel as a "cancer" that must be "eradicated," should thus be seen within this framework.[41]

Iran has suffered a severe blow due to the deterioration of the Assad regime in Syria, and it is not at all certain that it will turn its nuclear capabilities into nuclear arms. Iran can adopt a policy of nuclear ambiguity while persisting with its brinkmanship, allowing it to threaten the region and the U.S., as well as erode Israel's standing as one of the strongest countries in the region.

The question is where Iran is heading. Will it be satisfied with brinkmanship and a central role that influences the price of oil in the Organization of the Petroleum Exporting Countries (OPEC), and ensures economic development and a certain degree of influence on Iraqi politics, or will it strive to annex territory, transform regimes and take control of the Gulf's oil fields? Iran's conduct and the response of the West and the Gulf countries will largely determine the character of regional geopolitics: rivalry, cooperation or regional hegemony.

Israel is too small to pose a threat to Iran for a prolonged period of time. Turkey is geographically too far to currently interfere in the Persian Gulf, and the U.S. has adopted a cautious policy that prefers to react and adapt rather than be proactive. In another ten years, Turkey will be the only country in the region that can confront Iran, regardless of what the U.S. decides to do. Yet it is still unclear what path Turkey will choose.

The Rise of Turkish Power

Turkey is currently enjoying unprecedented economic growth. It is the seventeenth largest economy in the world, and the largest in the Middle East.[42] Its central geostrategic location between East and West and its strong army (which, excluding Russia and the United Kingdom, is the largest in Europe) make Turkey a major geopolitical actor in the Middle East.

---

[41] The speech from February 3, 2012. See: Economist, February 11th 2012.

[42] Lindenstrauss, 2011.

For a long period of time, Turkey strove to join the West and become a member of the EU. However, repeated rejections brought about a policy change in Turkey's geopolitical orientation as its decision-makers discovered the economic potential of the Middle East and Central Asia. At the same time, significant changes took place in Turkey's internal politics. Following the 9/11 attacks and the war in Iraq, which Turkey termed a war with Islam, it has seen a large rise in the number of Turks returning to religious life. There is also a significant rise in the number of those who perceive the U.S. as a military threat, and a decrease in the number of Turks who support joining the EU. Its increasingly religious and anti-Western orientation has been accompanied by the neutralization of the army's power, considered the guardian of secular life in Turkey, coupled with the appointment of Islamist officers and judges.[43] The 2011 election in Turkey saw a rise in the power of Erdogan's Justice and Development Party, which received fifty percent of the votes. Erdogan's victories and popularity have enabled his party to rule the country without the need for coalition partners.

As opposed to Iran, which imposes an authoritarian theocratic regime on its people, Turkey has introduced a dynamic model of growth and prosperity led by an Islamist party, which is successfully connecting what is considered a moderate form of Islam with processes of democratization. From this perspective, Turkey is a role model for Islamic movements vying for control in countries like Tunisia and Egypt. Although Turkey has avoided calling for Middle Eastern unification, some are convinced that once the wave of uprisings of the Arab Spring subsides, Turkey will be in a position to unite all the Sunni Muslim countries in the Middle East under one umbrella. With Iran isolated from the rest of the world due to growing concern in Sunni countries, and with Egypt's significance as a central strategic player weakened since it is coping with its problems at home, Israel is now seen by Turkey to be a prime strategic competitor.

It should come as no surprise that the Islamic government leading Turkey has chosen to end its strategic military alliance and reduce its diplomatic relations with Israel. It has become an ardent supporter of Hamas in Gaza, with the aim of gaining the religious Arab public on its side. Turkey criticizes Israel for the ongoing occupation of Palestinian lands; nevertheless the two countries enjoyed a strong alliance for years, despite the occupation. Turkey's support for the Palestinians and its popularity in the Arab world reached its zenith following the

---

[43] A fascinating debate on these issues appears in Cagaptay, 2010.

flotilla to Gaza in 2010, in which nine Turkish citizens aboard the Mavi Marmara were killed by Israeli forces.

The question is what Turkey will do next. Will it turn its back on the West and seek to become the leading power in the region? Will its detachment from the West be followed by a further deterioration of relations with Israel? It appears as if the EU rejection of Turkey's membership and the opening of Arab markets to Turkey are accelerating the process of detachment from the West.[44] Relations between Israel and Turkey are at an all-time low, and there is currently no Israeli ambassador stationed in Turkey. At the same time, Israel and other Western countries are trying to iron out the difficulties. Turkey is of vital importance to NATO due to its size, location and power. Turkey's criticisms of the Assad regime (an Iranian ally), the seizure of Iranian arms en route to Syria, cooperation with the West and support for Syrian opposition forces, as well as the cancellation of the second flotilla to Gaza, indicate that beyond the euphoria and reproach, there is also a sobering trend in both Israel and Turkey.

As far as America's geopolitical perspective is concerned, Turkey is one of the most important players in the region. It is therefore to be expected that the U.S. will make every effort to moderate the tensions between Turkey and Israel and try to restore good relations between the two. Advocates of this approach distinguish clearly between the tempestuous rhetoric of Turkish President Erdogan and Turkey's more pragmatic conduct.[45] If the effort succeeds, one can expect to see the formation of alliances modeled after the Cold War blocks: Turkey and Israel aligned with the West and Iran, China and Russia on the other side. Such a constellation would be indicative of the **return of the Cold War** at a regional scale, where the main focus is the region's resources and strategic positions.

If this effort fails, one can expect to see a new constellation in the Middle East based on new alliances and rivalries. In this case, Turkey will seek regional hegemony through the revival of a neo-Ottoman caliphate, which Iran will try to counter. Turkey will attempt to strengthen its power as a central player in the region between North Africa, the Middle East and the Balkans. One of its first steps would be to challenge Israel's status in the region and see how far the US is willing to go in supporting it. This affront will test American policy: Will the US government be willing to continue supporting Israel at the risk of damaging

---

[44] Walker and Alessandri, 2011.

[45] Kardas, 2011

ties with Turkey? Or will it prefer to support Turkey at the expense of its support for Israel?[46]

The first signs of such a test surfaced when Turkey threatened to send warships to Israeli gas-drilling areas in the eastern Mediterranean, to forcefully break the siege on Gaza and to support Lebanon in the event of a conflict with Israel. According to media leaks, Turkey's National Security Council has placed Israel in its "red book," listing it among the countries posing a threat to Turkish strategic interests in the region.[47]

What was supposed to be a Turkish policy of "zero problems with its neighbors" has quickly become a policy of "hostility in all directions." Western European countries are also affected by this new policy. Turkey made it clear to Cyprus that it must cease its gas drilling in an area Turkey claims to be under its sovereignty. Britain and France have been denounced for their alleged colonialist involvement in Libya. All these examples point to the fact that Turkey is planning to end its geopolitical pro-Western orientation and become an independent axis in the region.

These developments have led to increased suspicion in Israel. At the end of 2011, the Ministry of Defense instructed Israel's aviation industry and Elbit Systems Ltd. (a defense electronics manufacturer and integrators based in Haifa, Israel) to refrain from providing Turkey with an aerial intelligence system worth $141 million due to fears that completion of the deal would lead to the transmission of sensitive technology to Iran.[48]

In the meantime, Turkey is maintaining peaceful relations with Iran, *inter alia* because it cannot contend with it, and because it needs its oil. However, in the long term, Turkey may become a regional superpower that can contend with Iran. Turkey's economy is stronger and more dynamic than Iran's, and it can support a more sophisticated army. Turkey is also at a strategic geographic advantage, due to its ability to turn to the Balkans, the Caucasus, Central Asia and Mediterranean and North African countries - while Iran is isolated. Iran has never been a significant naval power, and because of its isolated ports and location, it will never be one in the future. Turkey, on the other hand, was for a long period the dominant power in the Middle East, and could reassume that position in the future. Turkey's goals and Iran's concerns about Turkey could lead to friction and clashes in the next decade. The rivalry between the two may lead to a nuclear

---

[46] Özel and Tuğtan. October 12, 2011.
[47] Los Angeles Times, November 1.
[48] Zeitun, December 22, 2011.

arms race, joined by Egypt, Syria and Saudi Arabia. One result may be a **regional balance of power** akin to the relations between superpowers in the region during the Cold War. Such a situation could guarantee long-term stability in the Middle East.

Another possible result is Turkish **regional hegemony** as it positions itself as the head of the Sunni axis by pushing Iran and the Shi'ite camp to the sidelines. Israel's participation in a Sunni axis may advance a solution to the Israeli-Palestinian conflict, backed by countries in this axis.

A third possible result is protracted **regional rivalry** between the countries that identify with the Sunni and Shi'ite axes. Israel and Egypt may play an important role in these axes and be sought after by the two sides for this reason. The most plausible option is that Israel will rebuild and strengthen its relations with Turkey, especially if the latter maintains its association with NATO and the West.

In each one of the four scenarios – return of the Cold war, balance of power, regional hegemony or regional rivalry – Turkey is destined to play a strategically important role due to its location between East and West, its economic power and its diplomatic ties. If Turkey wishes to become a hegemonic power in the region, it is bound to find itself in a conflict with Russia over regional influence in Central Asia and with America over its influence in the Middle East.

Geopolitical Implications for Israel

These regional developments are rife with uncertainties that are creating a sense of insecurity and instability in the region. The continued decline of American power may deepen these trends and place Israel in new and unpredictable situations. A new order in the Middle East characterized by Turkish hegemony may bring about regional stability, especially if this axis adopts a policy of reconciliation that maintains relations with the West. In this constellation, one can picture the advancement of the peace process between Israeli and Palestinians, backed by a moderate Sunni axis. However, a Sunni axis that is hostile towards Israel, which is dealing with a hostile Shi'ite force, will require that Israel intensify its reliance on the US and create new alliances with countries in southern Europe. Israel's strengthening of relations with Greece, Bulgaria and Romania is evidence of such a direction.

Theses geopolitical trends do not support hopes for the realization of a two-state solution based on the 1967 borders. They also do not indicate that agreements between Israel and Muslim and Arab countries within the framework of the 2002 Arab Peace Initiative are attainable in the foreseeable future. The initiative offers normalized relations between Israel and the Arab world on the basis of solving three key issues: borders between Israel and the Palestinian Authority; Jerusalem; and the Palestinian refugee problem according to Resolution 194 of 1948, which members of the Arab League have interpreted as allowing Palestinians to return to their former homes. However, the Initiative specifies the need for Israeli and Palestinian agreement on the issue, and thus opens up many possibilities.

The regional changes taking place cast doubt on the possible formation of a moderate Muslim axis. The rise of Islamist parties to power in Turkey, Egypt and Tunisia implies that even moderate forces may adopt anti-Israel policies in order to strengthen their strategic positions in the region. There is therefore no guarantee that these forces will operate to promote a peace process that brings about an agreed upon settlement between Israel and the Palestinian Authority. The behavior of these driving forces indicates the potential for a Middle East that is unstable, threatening and susceptible to erupting into war.

One of the most disconcerting problems facing the region is the severe vulnerability of the civil population following clashes that might turn into wars between countries or coalitions. While the population in the Middle East used to be mostly rural and scattered, today there is a high concentration of populations in large cities. The rapid process of urbanization in the Middle East, along with industrialization and the concentration of infrastructures and energy facilities in a small number of locations, implies a high rate of civilian casualties in the event of war. This reality may act as a moderating force in any war, but could also be a tempting factor. The next war, if and when it breaks out, will likely be concentrated in cities and around infrastructures that can lead to high fatality rates. Naturally, this fact heavily influences the outlining of Israel's borders. The proximity of a hostile army to large population centers in Israel could increase the number of civilian casualties. Thus it is fair to expect that in the face of these threatening scenarios, Israel will make sure to maintain defensible borders.

The Local Level: Internal Processes in Arab Countries; Unrest, Uncertainty and Insecurity

The Middle East is in the midst of economic, cultural, religious and social upheaval accompanied by a decline in the legitimacy of regimes, the ousting of autocratic rulers and the rise of new ideologies (See Illustration 8). These processes, characterized as the "Arab Spring," portend a period of instability, uncertainty and insecurity. They reflect internal developments in the Arab world that are disconnected from the Israeli-Palestinian conflict, yet have an effect on Israel.

Will the Arab Spring and the removal of autocrats lead to a democratic summer of stability and moderation, or will it end in an autumn of national-religious regimes and even deteriorate into a winter of radical regimes hostile to democracy and human rights? Democracy and moderation can assist in promoting a solution to the conflict between Israel and the Palestinian Authority, while hostility may lead Israel to entrench itself further in its own positions.

Illustration 8: Possible developments in the Arab World

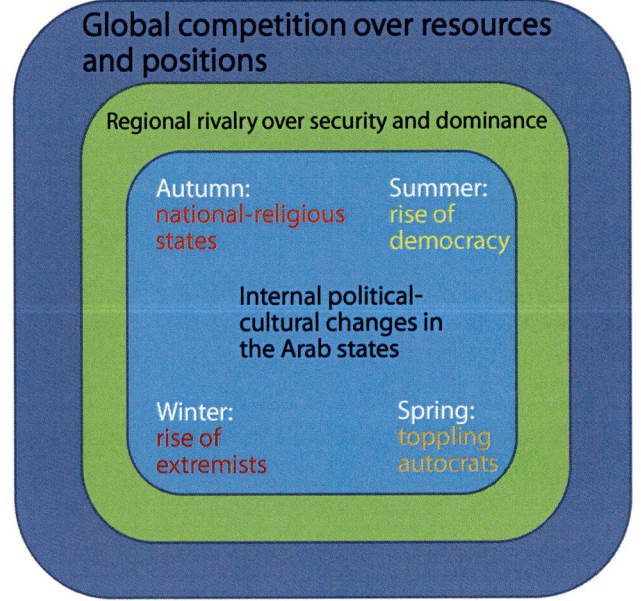

There is no doubt that calls for the elimination of corruption, for social justice and for freedom reflect a genuine grassroots democratic process that seeks to restore the public's honor and justice.[49] However, there is no guarantee that the democratic uprising will immediately transform into a democratic regime. Projecting the future requires a broad geographical and historical outlook that

---

[49] See Ajami, 2012 and: a public opinion poll in five Arab countries conducted by Shibley Telhami, 2011. Most of those polled said the Arab Spring is an essential expression of the striving for honor, liberty and prosperity.

relates to deep-seated political and social structures, cultural norms and differences between countries in the region. Firstly, it should be noted that no wave of protest has spread in a uniform fashion: The leaders who were deposed all ruled republics, while the monarchs managed to remain in place, despite their power being challenged. Secondly, the ousting of the autocrats in the republics does not translate into substantial change in demographic, economic or social processes or in the political and social norms at the root of the upheaval. Finally, the rise to power of Islamic-oriented parties casts a long shadow over the democratic outlook of the new regimes. It currently looks as if the Arab Spring is immersed in deep uncertainty, and it will require a protracted period of transition till things become clear.[50]

Demography, Economy and Society

The processes of demographic growth and the migration from the countryside to the city in Arab and Muslim countries have led to high demand for housing, employment and services. The result is a wide gap between the supply and demand for jobs, and a sharp rise in housing prices and other consumer goods. Unemployment rates are rising, reaching a third of the workforce, and inflation is skyrocketing.

Governments are finding it hard to deal with these problems and are vulnerable to increasing criticism by the public. This criticism is coming primarily from the young generation, and especially those that have made the move to the city, acquired an education, are well-versed in advanced communication technologies and social media, and are aware of the political and economic processes taking place in the world. The demographic data in the Arab world clearly show that despite the remarkable decline in births, nearly half of the population is under 25 years old. There is no guarantee that the removal of authoritarian regimes will solve these problems, and it is likely that they will only become worse if the new political powers choose to cut off ties and reduce economic cooperation with the West. The rise of Islamic-oriented governments that are hostile to democratic processes may generate severe disappointment among the younger, more modern population and deepen criticism of the regimes. The instability is also worsening as a result of the tribal nature of Arab society, as well as the explicit ethnic and

---

[50] An excellent source on the demographic, social and economic trends in the Middle East is the Rand Center's paper on sources of conflict in the Middle East. See Lesser, Nardulli, Arghavan, 1998.

religious divisions in countries like Syria, Lebanon, Libya, Saudi Arabia, Yemen, Egypt and Bahrain.

Religion

Criticism of the authoritarian regimes by the young, modernizing generation has found advocates and partners in the Islamic movements, which aim to implement theocratic rule in the state. These movements provide services to those villagers who have made it to the city and, in the process, transmit their religious messages and strengthen their political power. This has resulted in increased political criticism from both the social democratic national perspective and the religious national perspective. These criticisms are currently integrated; however it is possible there will be internal power struggles in the future.

At this point, the Islamic parties have achieved political representation and influence. The moderate Islamist Ennahda Movement in Tunisia won 40 percent of the votes in recent elections, while the rest were distributed among the secular parties. In Egyptian parliamentary elections, the Muslim Brotherhood and the Salafist Movement's Al-Nour Party won almost 70 percent of all votes, and together control the parliament. In addition, Mohamed Morsi, a member of the Muslim Brotherhood, was elected as president. The key question is how the Islamic parties will address the calls for democratization: Will they reject them, or try to find channels that enable the simultaneous pursuit of Islamic rule and democracy? The answers will greatly affect relations with the young, modern generation that protested in the streets and demanded regime change. Relations with the public will also be influenced by how economic issues are dealt with. Without addressing the demographic and economic problems, the public at large, and in particular those who supported the Islamic parties, are likely to become disillusioned and return to the streets. Another question is how the army will respond and whom it will prefer to ally with. It may prefer a coalition of liberal players or one of the Islamic players. No conclusions can yet be reached as to what is going to happen in the future in countries such as Egypt, Tunisian or Libya.

Technology

Opposition movements confronting their regimes are benefiting from the ongoing technological revolution. Khomenei used to transmit his sermons via cassette tapes, then through fax machines and today – as was evident from the demonstrations in Tunisia, Egypt, Syria and Libya – people are using smartphones, Facebook,

Skype and Twitter. New information technologies have paved the way for an effective and continuous flow of information and help in enlisting support. These tools also serve religious organizations that seek to disseminate their messages. Information technologies have enabled the rapid spread of protests and struggles from country to country. The democratic process being enacted in urban squares has become a prominent phenomenon circulated by the media to the various cities of the Middle East. At the same time, there is no substitute for leadership or organizational capacities. The youth who captured the world's attention in Tahrir Square have not succeeded politically. Opposition forces in Syria, which have been conveying agonizing descriptions of the Syrian army's brutal behavior, have not been able to unite and form a coherent leadership.

Regime Change

The toppling of authoritarian regimes in Tunisia, Egypt and Libya as well as the conflicts taking place in Syria, Yemen, and Bahrain indicate that such regimes have reached their end. The question is what kind of government will replace them in the republics, and what will happen in the monarchies. It is especially interesting to see how things will develop in Egypt, which may determine how trends develop in the rest of the region.

There are several types of regimes that may emerge in the future, from democratic to radical, fundamentalist ones. Some foresee democratic regimes in Tunisia, Libya and Egypt, and a long period of conflicts in Syria, Yemen, and Bahrain. Others believe that after a short period of democracy demonstrated by free elections, radical Islamic forces will take over. In the meantime, the future character of these regimes, their ideals and values, remains unclear. It seems as if unifying ideals such as the fight against colonialism, pan-Arabism and the non-aligned policy have exhausted themselves. What will replace them? In the absence of unifying ideals, it seems likely that there will be a long period of internal rivalries, instability and yearning for a strong leader who will restore order. Is Israel's designation as enemy and a call for changing the peace agreements destined to be part of these unifying ideologies?

Ideology

One option is that the ruling ideology will be based on a combination of nationalism and Islam. Islam rules in Iran, Algeria (at one point, but was removed by the army), Turkey and the Palestinian Authority (but deposed and moved to Gaza),

Lebanon (the strengthening of Hezbollah), Tunisia and Egypt. This ideology is likely to take hold in Syria if Bashar al-Assad is deposed. The Islamic parties are not cut from the same cloth. They range from moderate parties looking to build alliances with the West, like Turkey's Justice and Development Party, to radical governments like the one ruling Iran, which is in direct confrontation with the West.

Nationalism may also play an important role in rallying the public behind the new regimes. Unlike Europe, the Middle East is still in the process of creating a nation-state, undergoing a transition from a tribal to a national society. National conflicts, and in particular the conflict with Israel, may serve as an important tool for nation building. The possibility of a linkage between Islam and nationalism, as happened in Lebanon, Turkey and Iran, should not be ruled out.

As opposed to pan-Islamism, which is meta-nationalist, political Islam may contribute to the deepening of nationalism, inter alia, by improving the welfare system, rooting out corruption, extending religious control and emphasizing national rivalries. This form of political Islam could intensify border conflicts, spread intolerance towards minorities, and bring about alliances based on religious nationalism. The conflict with Israel can play a central role in this new identity, due to the fact that the Israeli-Palestinian conflict is considered a central problem in the Arab world. Paradoxically, the democratization process, which seeks to express the public view, could swing the pendulum in a direction hostile to Israel. Democratization may eventually lead Egypt, and later Jordan, to reconsider their peace agreements with Israel.

Geopolitical Implications for Israel

The economic, political and social developments taking place in Arab countries are shrouded in uncertainty. In the short term, one can expect unrest and the manifestation of three primary ideologies: nationalism, democracy and Islamism.

The democratization process, adoption of human rights and protection of minorities may contribute to the moderation of tensions between Israel and its neighbors. In such conditions, Israel would need to demonstrate goodwill towards the moderate forces by reaching an agreement with the Palestinian Authority. At the same time, the democratization process cannot be expected to take place overnight. A long transition period should be taken into account, throughout which there may be many ups and downs, as has happened in past revolutions.

The military may assume control for a period of time and try and maintain authoritarian rule. The military's involvement in the economy is a good reason to preserve existing patterns. An interim agreement would allow Israel to evaluate the trends and prepare accordingly.

Increasing nationalism accompanied by acquiescence to populist anti-Israel sentiments could aggravate relations between Israel and its neighbors. The combination of nationalism and Islamism in bordering countries would prove dangerous for Israel. Under such circumstances, it is difficult to foresee any progress towards a peace process or even towards an interim agreement. The two most likely options are remaining in the territories or withdrawing to defensible borders.

Relations between Israel and the Palestinian Authority

The relationship between Israel and the Palestinian Authority is affected by several internal factors: Government power, public opinion, the power of peace spoilers (those opposing a peace agreement) and demographic processes taking place between the Jordan River and the Mediterranean (See Illustration 9).[51]

Illustration 9: The forces shaping relations between Israel and the Palestinian Authority

---

[51] Hasson, Ben-Bassat, Halevy, Neeman, Newman, Sabel, Sela, Feitelson, 2011.

Governments' Strength

In recent years, the relations between Israel and the Palestinian Authority have been in an unprecedented calm. The two entities are engaged in security cooperation to prevent terror. Economic growth in Israel and the Palestinian Authority is impressive. Despite the global economic crisis, Israel has been enjoying relative stability and one of the highest rates of growth among developed countries (between four and five percent). High rates of growth have been registered in the West Bank and Gaza (six and nine percent, respectively), largely thanks to outside grants and the calculated economic and security policies enacted by Prime Minister Salam Fayyad. This is an important breakthrough in relations between Israel and the Palestinian Authority. Instead of nurturing the conflict, the Palestinian Authority is focused on building the institutions, infrastructure and economy necessary for a state. Both sides have taken important steps to build trust, including the Israeli prime minister's declaration of support for a two-state solution.

There are nevertheless a number of factors preventing progress towards an agreement. One is the political divide between the West Bank governed by Fatah and the Hamas-governed Gaza Strip. As opposed to the Fayyad government in the West Bank, which is striving to maintain security and advance economic development, the Hamas government led by Ismail Haniyeh is waging a constant war against Israel. Gaza is a haven for the Islamic Jihad and other Jihadi organizations, and is arming itself with advanced weaponry that poses a threat to communities deep inside Israel. It is hard to imagine Israel reaching an agreement with the Fayyad government when it is under attack by the Hamas and Islamic Jihad in Gaza. The reconciliation process between Fatah and Hamas is stuck. It seems as if Hamas's political leadership, which resided outside Gaza, wishes to advance reconciliation; however Hamas leaders in Gaza refuse to give up their political and economic power and are thus thwarting reconciliation.

The main barrier on the road to peace, however, is not an internal Palestinian divide, but rather the unique character of the Israeli-Palestinian conflict. As opposed to the conflicts with other Arab countries, this one is heavily loaded with symbolic issues. One of the main problems is the issue of Jerusalem. Any concession could ignite internal strife in which the diasporas on both sides will be deeply involved.

Another sensitive issue is the refugees. The Palestinians cannot give up on this issue, which forms a central component of their national identity. The unwillingness to make concession on this issue is perceived in Israel as a refusal to recognize Israel as the national homeland of the Jewish people. This explains the symbolic nature of the conflict, at the heart of which is Israel's demand to be recognized as a Jewish nation-state.

Although in 1988 Palestinians accepted UN Resolution 181 of 1947, regarding the division of Palestine into an Arab state and a Jewish state, they still refuse to recognize Israel as the nation-state of the Jewish people. This refusal is explained by their contention that recognition would render the history of the Palestinian struggle illegitimate, undermine the Palestinian right of return, and harm the rights of those Arabs living in Israel. Even inside Israel there are disputes about the demand and some claim that the citizens themselves should be the ones to determine Israel's character as a Jewish nation-state – thereby deeming it unnecessary for the Palestinian Authority to do so. The pragmatic approach claims that Israel can conduct itself as a Jewish nation-state and prevent the return of Palestinian refugees as long as it maintains the necessary power. The moment it loses that power, Palestinian recognition will not be of any value anyway. Israel has reacted to the Palestinian refusal to recognize it as a Jewish state by continuing to build settlements in the West Bank. Palestinians, in turn, have refused to conduct direct negotiations with Israel.

The question is whether the current state of calm is stable and well-balanced. What could support a progress towards an agreement, and what could cause the situation to deteriorate and make an agreement even more remote? The answer is highly dependent on the power of governments on both sides, and primarily on their willingness and capability to sign an agreement and see it through. Historical processes until now demonstrate that both governments have failed to respect signed agreements. At the same time, in recent years the Palestinian Authority has been a stable regime striving for economic development and maintaining law and order throughout the West Bank. Through cooperation with Israel, this government has managed to guarantee peace and security across the West Bank. Within this context, the Palestinian government led by Salam Fayyad and Mahmoud Abbas is the best partner Israel has ever had.

However, at the same time, there are no diplomatic ties between the governments, nor any negotiations about reaching a solution. Israel continues to build settlements, and the Palestinian Authority has unilaterally turned to the UN Security Council and then to the General Assembly to be recognized as an independent state.

Public Opinion

Israeli and Palestinian public opinion is largely supportive of a two-state solution but is simultaneously convinced there is no possibility to achieve an agreement due to a lack of trust. An Israeli-Palestinian poll conducted in December 2011 demonstrates that 58 percent of Israelis and 50 percent of Palestinians support the 2000 Clinton Parameters, as expressed in the 2003 Geneva Initiative, outlining two states for two peoples. At the same time, 53 percent of Israelis and 63 percent of Palestinians believe the other side opposes such an agreement.[52] It is a state of cognitive dissonance in which each side holds contradicting positions about the future solution. This dissonance reflects the deep lack of trust between the two sides and their tendency to avoid taking any risks. Both sides attribute greater importance to the risks involved in failing to conclude an agreement than to the opportunities that may stem from such an agreement. In recent years, increased pessimism has become apparent on both sides. Polls show that a majority of two-thirds on both sides is convinced that it is impossible to reach a permanent agreement at this time, and that the chance for the establishment of an independent Palestinian state alongside Israel is minuscule.[53] Israelis tend to lean more to the right, doubtful of the chance for a solution, while more and more Palestinians do not believe there is a chance for a two-state solution and opt for a bi-national state. At the same time international legitimacy for Israel is dwindling, especially among young, liberal and educated people in the West. But for the time being this seems to have a little impact on public opinion and governmental conduct in Israel.

Peace Spoilers: Extremist Non-State Actors

There are extremist organizations on both sides that oppose an agreement: settler groups on the one hand and Hamas and other Islamic movements on the other. The coalition in Israel provides significant power and support for the settlers. This support originates in Shas, other religious parties and Israel Beiteinu, which brings together Russian-Israelis and rightwing parties. On the other side, the split between Hamas and Fatah has provided the former a kind of veto power over the pursuit of the peace process. This right is realized through the barrage of rockets inflicted on the south of Israel. It is difficult to imagine the pursuit of a peaceful solution under the constant threat of missiles striking Israeli towns.

---

[52] PSR - Survey Research Unit, 2011.

[53] Ibid.

Future developments may see the rise of even more radical non-state actors, such as international terror cells possessing advanced arms. Under such conditions, even agreements with Hamas will not withstand the threat of terror, because such groups can sabotage any agreement signed.

Demographic Processes[54]

Demographic processes are undermining the current Jewish majority between the Mediterranean and the Jordan. In 2010, there were 11,455,000 people living in this territory, of which 6,017,000 were Jews, 5,206,000 Arabs and 313,000 others. The Jewish population formed a majority in the region, although a tiny one: 52.6 percent. The continuation of demographic trends characterized by high Muslim fertility rates as compared with Jewish rates foreshadows an Arab majority in the near future.

---

[54] DellaPergola, 2011.

THE SCENARIOS

A review of the driving forces indicates a strong connection between developments in the Middle East and possible developments in the Israeli-Palestinian conflict. The major question is how developments in both areas affect each other. Can the Israeli-Palestinian conflict be resolved without settling the wider regional conflict? How will an unresolved Israeli-Palestinian conflict affect developments in the region?

Literature dealing with the Israeli-Palestinian conflict tends to focus on the local arena, while the literature dealing with Middle East processes tends to focus solely on the regional and global levels. The result is disjointed scenarios at different geographic levels. Thus, for example, in the late 1990s, researchers at the Rand Corporation developed several scenarios regarding the future developments in the Middle East in 2025. These scenarios offer many important insights into what could happen in the area. Some described the collapse of the regime in Egypt and the rise of Turkey as a leading regional power; however, they do not thoroughly examine the influences of these developments on the Israeli-Palestinian conflict and the ensuing possible future borders.[55] The scenarios developed by the Rand Corporation lay out four different strategic worlds in the Middle East: **Great Game,** in which the primary driving force is regional rivalry and the main conflict is over resources and territories; **Clash of Civilizations,** in which the primary driving force is a religious conflict between Islam and the West, as outlined by Samuel Huntington; **Anarchy,** in which the primary driving forces are the internal economic, religious and tribal rivalries; **End of History**, in which the central driving forces are democratization and creation of a new world order, as envisaged by Francis Fukuyama, leading to ideological convergence and security.

The National Intelligence Council (NIC) in the United States offers several global scenarios that relate to the Middle East. These scenarios examine possible future trends, and suggest the possible futures of "A new caliphate", "Pax Americana" and the "Cycle of fear."[56] The NIC, together with the European Union Institute for Security Studies, has developed one of the most recent papers

---

[55] See Rand scenarios about global strategic alternatives and their implications for the Middle East: Lesser, Nardulli and Arghavan, 1998, p.217.
[56] See the NIC scenarios on the global developments projected in 2020: NIC, 2004.

addressing future scenarios at the global level.[57] This paper identifies three chief driving forces that will shape the world order: mutual dependence, the emergence of a multifocal world, and the rise of non-state players. Relying on these three driving forces, four global scenarios are suggested for 2025: "Barely keeping afloat," which is a continuation of business as usual; "Fragmentation" – a scenario of relatively closed blocs while slowing down the processes of globalization; "Concert of Europe Redux", which foresees the strengthening of global cooperation and coordination; and "Gaming Reality: Conflict Trumps Cooperation" – a scenario in which the current reality of cooperation is replaced by conflict. These are global scenarios that do not directly address the Israeli-Palestinian conflict, but rather reflect the U.S. outlook and interests as an empire with a global perspective.

Several other scenarios have been developed by Israeli and Palestinian think tanks which focus directly on the Israeli-Palestinian conflict, analyzing possible future relations between Israel and the Palestinian Authority.[58] Quite often these scenarios tend to emphasize what each side desires and not necessarily what is possible. For example, the Palestine Strategy Group (PSG) produced such a set of scenarios. They underscore how Israeli-Palestinian relations rarely relate to global and regional processes. The four scenarios preferred by the PSG are: a two-state solution that provides a just solution to the refugee problem; a binational state; a state of all its citizens; and a confederation between an independent Palestinian state and Jordan. The undesired scenarios are the continuation of the status quo, a Palestinian state with interim borders, unilateral disengagement undertaken by Israel and the partition of the West Bank and Gaza between Jordan and Egypt.[59]

This distinction between desired and undesired is significant, but does not address the central question guiding the development of scenarios: What are the actual processes and trends and what kind of reality are they leading towards? Obviously, these processes are influenced by many factors over which neither Israelis nor Palestinians have full control. It is possible that an outline of borders will emerge that is not necessarily desired by the two sides. A protracted regional conflict could, for example, delay the solution to the conflict and leave the situation as it is, despite being undesired by both sides.

---

[57] National Intelligence Council and EU Institute for Security Studies, 2010.

[58] One of the pioneer studies in this field is: Yariv, Alpher, Feldman, Ben-Meir, Ben-Zvi, Eytan, Gazit, Gold, Heller, Karsh, Kurz, Levite, Meir, Peri, and Shalev, 1989.

[59] See Palestine Strategy Group, 2011.

A noted attempt to transcend the desired vision while taking into account regional and local developments is offered by the Shasha Center for Strategic Studies.[60] Unlike other scenarios that assumed a business as usual approach and failed to see the coming regime change in the Arab world, the scenarios developed by the Shasha Center expected the rise to power of the Islamic movement in Egypt.[61]

To create a synthesis between macro and micro scenarios one has to examine the reciprocal relations between developments at the global, regional and national levels. Specifically, one has to analyze the processes taking place at the level of the superpowers, relations within and between countries in the Middle East, and relations between Israel and the Palestinian Authority. Several journalists and public figures have sketched outlines for such scenarios.[62] However, a study has yet to be done that systematically examines the relation between developments on various levels while relating to social, economic, political, security and geopolitical processes. Such a study requires interdisciplinary cooperation that cuts across geographic boundaries, connects diverse fields of thought while bringing together researchers and practitioners. The following pages present a conceptual sketch for this kind of research.

---

[60] The Shasha Center for Strategic Studies' think tank identified the critical driving forces, clarified their uncertainty, and examined the relations between them. See: Hasson, Ben-Bassat, Halevy, Neeman, Newman, Sabel, Sela, Feitelson, 2011.

[61] In a strategic assessment on the future of Egypt written on the eve of the Arab Spring in 2010, Yoram Meital wrote: "The primary significance that emerges from the aforementioned scenarios is that to the chagrin of those in the opposition, the rules of the political game in Egypt will not change, and the chances of one of their candidates taking the presidency is unrealistic....The mechanisms of power and security guarantee continuation of governing structures in Egypt, however this is not supported by the public at large." See Meital, 2010, p.160-61.

[62] In February, 2011, Rula Khaalaf thus described three meta-scenarios for Egypt: Continuation of Mubarak rule, the assumption of power by the army and the formation of a unity government comprised of the opposition movements. See Khaalaf, February 1, 2011. Mohamed Hassanein Heikal presented more in-depth scenarios in Al Ahram's weekly magazine, which identify four main players: The West, Turkey, Iran and Israel. It presents two scenarios. One is the takeover of the Middle East by the West through encouraging continued conflict between Sunnis and Shi'ites and the takeover of strategic areas and oil sources under the guise of aiding the Sunni population. In this scenario, the Muslim Brotherhood is not aware of this strategy and cooperates with the West, as Egypt loses its position as an important strategic player. Most of the attention turns to internal political issues. In the second scenario, the one preferred by Heikal, a regional bloc is formed in which the Sunni Muslim world softens its hatred towards Iran and its doubts regarding Turkey and stands up to the West. See: Ezzat, September 29-October 5, 2011.

Four Scenarios and Israel's Geopolitical Dilemma

Four primary scenarios emerge from the analysis of the driving forces. Each scenario provides a different solution to Israel's geopolitical dilemma, which reflects various global, regional and national developments and different relations between the driving forces (See Illustration 10).

Illustration 10: Four Scenarios

Scenario 1: "Pax Americana" and a Return to the 1967 Borders

In this scenario, the U.S. manages to restore its ability to steer and lead the Middle East, and succeeds in impeding the rise of local powers seeking regional hegemony, as well as the reemergence of Russia and the rise of China. The traditional strategic axis between Israel and Turkey has been restored and is joined by Egypt and Jordan. Turkey has proven its commitment to NATO by agreeing to position radars against missiles in its territory, which are designed to protect European countries and moderate the tension with Israel. It is a clear indication that Turkey has not abandoned its connections to the West, and is not looking to strengthen ties with Iran. Iran's power has significantly declined due to regime change in Syria and the rise of a moderate Islamic regime. The Arab Spring is transforming into a summer in which democratic ruling forces are interested in negotiating with Israel towards an end to the Israeli-Palestinian conflict. Hamas's power is consequently undermined as it is increasingly seen as a militant and authoritarian organization that violates basic human rights and democracy.

Israel is governed by a moderate coalition that wishes to change the geopolitical situation and has the capacity to take action. In the Palestinian Authority Fatah has the upper hand in its struggle with Hamas, enjoying support from the young generation. The new government takes steps towards stabilization and economic development, as well as strengthening democratic processes through security coordination with Israel. These developments are prompting the Israeli and Palestinian governments to take risks never taken before. Public opinion on both sides also supports an agreement and tends to believe the promises being made by the other side, partly due to security and economic guarantees provided by the United States.

The process of democratization taking place in the region - the stabilization of the regimes and the formation of a strategic axis supported by the U.S. - are stimulating unprecedented economic growth. Israel and the Palestinian state, which have signed a permanent agreement, are becoming the central engine behind this growth, thanks to their human capital. Economic cooperation between Israelis and Palestinians blur the geopolitical borders and highlight the importance of collaboration that cuts across borders. This is especially evident in Jerusalem, where the most controversial areas are turning into centers of economic cooperation.

The role of the U.S. is primarily to support the agreements by providing economic dividends and by preventing radical actors from undermining them. As opposed to Obama's vision, which argued that an agreement between Israel and Palestine would ensure regional change, it is in fact the regional change that enables an agreement. The key to realizing this scenario is regional security, processes of democratization, tolerance, mutual trust and a pledge by the strongest superpower in the world and the region. A solution along the 1967 borders is possible as a result of regional stability and American peace in the Middle East, which provides security guarantees and ensures political and economic stability.

The chief problem with this optimistic scenario is how to actually make it happen when most of the signs are pointing in the opposite direction: The weakening of the U.S. position in the region, the rise of Islamic regimes in Arab countries, protracted economic instability in those countries associated with widening social gaps, the rise of Islam as a regional power and the weakening of the Palestinian Authority. In other words, what mechanism could ignite the process described in this scenario?

The developments outlined in the scenario may be realized due to **diplomatic processes** based upon dialogue and political and economic agreement between the U.S. and new regimes in the Middle East. The U.S. will recognize Islamic regimes in Egypt, Tunisia, and in the future, in Syria and even Jordan as well. It will support them financially and rebuild its geopolitical positioning in the region. Through diplomacy, the U.S. will moderate the radical tendencies of Islamic parties and nurture moderate Islamic regimes that are oriented towards democracy and reform. American support for processes of democratization in the region and criticism of Syria on the one hand, and Iranian, Russian and Chinese support for Assad's regime on the other, may assist in strengthening the U.S. presence in the region. The U.S. may also attempt to do what currently seems unimaginable: try to forge agreements with Iran based on an ambiguous nuclear capacity out of an understanding that it cannot fully stop Iran from developing nuclear weapons. If this happens, the level of anxiety in Gulf States, in Israel and even among America's Western allies will definitely increase. Nonetheless, establishing such understandings with Iran could reap economic and political dividends for the U.S. due to the strengthening of ties with the largest power in the Middle East.

If this policy fails due to the rise of extremist Islamic regimes and the increased threats to America's position in the Middle East by Iran with the backing of China and Russia, the U.S. will be forced to protect its interests in the region by confronting those challenging its position. The despair stemming from the failure to negotiate and forge agreements will be accompanied by a transition **from diplomatic processes to military action, which will include containment and confrontation with Iran in key geo-strategic areas, while increasing the reliance on countries under threat.** The U.S. can in fact use Iran's development of nuclear weapons to leverage its position in the region. Arab countries under threat, including Saudi Arabia and the Gulf States, will cooperate with the U.S. towards the effort to stop Iran and reduce its influence in the region. Israel could play a key role in this scenario by threatening Iran. These threats could propel diplomatic actions and sanctions against Iran and lead to an American-led coalition against it.

It is a sophisticated game of maintaining a balance of power in the region, which serves the interests of the U.S. On the one hand, Iran is on the brink of achieving nuclear weapons, and on the other, a superpower joined by Arab countries and Turkey which are under threat, and Israel. Such a situation serves U.S. interests in the Middle East, and indirectly serves Israel's as well. If such a situation persists for a long period of time, the U.S. can take advantage of its bolstered position in the region and exert pressure on Israel to return to negotiations and reach a solution based on the 1967 borders.

If Iran proceeds to develop nuclear weapons, threatens its neighbors and closes the Straits of Hormuz, the U.S. will have a pretense to strike Iran. Such an attack will not be limited to the nuclear facilities, which Iran could rebuild within a short period of time due to its scientific and technological capacity. It will require the deployment of ground forces that can penetrate infrastructures and target key leaders. Such an act will be supported by Saudi Arabia and the Gulf States, as well as EU member states, but will be condemned by China and Russia. These two countries will do everything in their power to propel the U.S. into a protracted conflict that will diminish its power. This could result in a regional war, in which Iran would enjoy support from Russia and China. The window of opportunity for such a war is extremely narrow. From the moment Iran has the capacity to develop a nuclear weapon, the chances for such an attack on it become increasingly low. In the event that Iran possesses such a weapon, it becomes an unpredictable country. On the one hand, there is the Shi'ite tradition of rationality and balance, and on the other hand, the isolation of Iran and the extremism of its religious leadership may push it to dangerous behavior. This would not only pose risks for Israel but also for the entire region and the world.

The key question is Turkey's position with regards to these diplomatic and military developments. A powerful Iran with nuclear weapons that joins forces with extremist Islamic regimes could lead Turkey to strengthen its alliance with the U.S. In this case, the U.S. could support Turkey in becoming a leading regional counter-power to Iran. At the same time, the U.S. may choose to distance itself from Israel, especially if Israel continues its current policy of refusing to reach any compromise with the Palestinian Authority. Such a move will be gradual. There will not be any drastic cuts in security budgets; however the U.S. would move the Israeli-Palestinian issue to the bottom of its agenda and inform Israel that it has no interest in forcing a solution on it. Such a statement would mark the beginning of American detachment from Israel as it improves relations with Turkey and the Muslim world. Israel will need to manage its geopolitical policy carefully in order to maintain its strategic alliance with the U.S., even if this means withdrawal from the territories and a return to the 1967 borders.

In both the diplomatic and the military strategies, America's chief goal is to ensure its own vital strategic and economic interests in the Middle East and those of its allies. Israel will have to contribute its part and make necessary territorial concessions. In other words, reaching an agreement based on the 1967 borders with land swaps will be in Israel's interest, especially if it seeks to maintain its position as an American ally. Israel's geopolitical policy regarding the borders will be largely dictated by global and regional developments. Continued American weakness and military and diplomatic failures will lead to the rise of other forces, including Turkey and Iran.

Scenario 2: Islamic Caliphate and Interim Borders between Israel and the Palestinian Authority

In this scenario, the U.S. demonstrates continued weakness. Its geopolitical decline will create a vacuum filled by an axis of Sunni countries – whether radical or moderate – led by Turkey, which seeks to revive a neo-Ottoman caliphate in the region. Establishment of a Sunni axis will lead to a confrontation between Iran and Turkey over regional hegemony. Iran is strengthening its position by forming alliances with the Shi'ite communities throughout the Middle East, including Iraq as well as Lebanon. It will foment rebellion by the Shi'ite populations in Bahrain, Kuwait and Saudi Arabia, and act to lure Syria in its direction. Turkey will strengthen its standing in the second decade of the 21st century by competing with Israel over positions of power in the eastern Mediterranean, and over opposition to Iran in the following decade.

An Iranian takeover of the Persian Gulf and the Arabian Peninsula clashes with Turkey's interests, which needs regional oil and wants to avoid relying on Russia for it. Turkey is thus likely to oppose an Iranian presence in Syria and Lebanon, which it regards as economic partners. This explains Turkey's support of opposition forces in Syria and its willingness to enable open and protected buffer zones on its borders. This is not aimed just at Syria but at Iran, which is the chief supporter of the Syrian regime headed by Assad. In the following decade, the Iranians will be forced to allocate numerous resources in order to deal with a rising Turkey. The Sunni Arab world will seek a country that can lead the region and confront Shi'ite Iran - and in spite of the history of strained relations between the Arab world and the Ottoman Empire, Sunni Turkey is the best candidate. According to a public opinion poll conducted in five Arab countries surveying which two countries played the most positive role in the Arab Spring, Turkey was the overwhelming choice. Half of those questioned specified its constructive contribution and when Egyptians were asked which of the leaders they want the next president of Egypt to emulate, 40% selected Erdogan.[63] Ahmadinejad came second with a tenth of the votes of those polled. This sympathy positions Turkey at an advantage as a leader in the Muslim world. In the coming confrontation with Iran over regional support, Turkey will have the upper hand.

Turkey's well-established economic position, its geopolitical influence on the Balkans, the Caucasus and the Middle East, the identification of Sunni countries with Turkey and their rejection of Shi'ite Iran will all work to secure its success. Turkey's transformation into a leading superpower will not happen overnight. It will encounter opposition from Egypt and Saudi Arabia, which see themselves as the epicenters of Sunni Islam. However, the enhanced Iranian threat, coupled with the economic crisis in Egypt, will increase the need for a regional solution and lead to the strengthening of ties with Turkey.

Another supporting factor is Turkey's ability to have a democratic-Islamic government that directly challenges the extremist Islamic regime in Iran. Turkey is thus in a position to form a strategic alliance with Egypt and Syria, thereby improving its relations with the Palestinian Authority. The rivalry between Turkey and Iran may result in a protracted conflict, or a balance of power in which both sides seek to develop nuclear capabilities and regional alliances. The possibility of cooperation between the two would lead to another scenario: A clash of civilizations (See Scenario 4).

The social and political unrest in Arab countries will end and a stable national-religious government will take hold. At first, the Palestinian Authority will refuse to negotiate with Israel and persist in its effort to attain international recognition at the United Nations. Israel on its part will refuse to negotiate with a Palestinian Authority reconciling with Hamas. However, developments in the Arab world may change the outlook of both sides. The rise of a Sunni coalition that confronts Iran and the election of an Islamic party in Egypt that upholds the peace treaty with Israel could contribute to the moderation of Hamas and its political agenda.[64] As the more moderate elements in the organization become stronger, Hamas may take the reins of power within the Palestinian Authority. Under such conditions, Hamas will suggest an interim agreement – a *hudna* – that does not prevent either

---

[63] See Arab world public opinion poll: Telhami, 2011.
[64] This paragraph was written about a year before Israel's Pillar of Defense operation in Gaza on November, 2012.

side from envisaging far-reaching ideological dreams while reaching pragmatic agreements that foster short and medium-term stability.

The Arab countries that comprise the Sunni axis will be sensitive to public opinion, especially public criticism of Israel's continued occupation. Those countries will offer Israel once again the chance to approve the Arab League Initiative by guaranteeing that a return to 1967 borders will facilitate reconciliation between Israel and the Muslim and Arab world. Countries that are part of this Sunni axis will participate in such an offer, with Turkey leading. Hamas will understand the offer as a *hudna* that does not imply an end to the conflict. It will not waive its historical claim concerning the right of return of Palestinian refugees to places like Jaffa and Haifa. Under such conditions Israel will have to decide whether it prefers to be part of a new Middle East, or continue its rejection of the Arab League Initiative. Israel's rejection of the Arab Peace Initiative will prompt Egypt and Jordan to reconsider their peace treaties. On the other hand, Israeli acceptance of the initiative could lead to reconciliation with the Arab world without a permanent resolution to the Israeli-Palestinian conflict (see upper left quarter of Illustration 10).

Israel will be facing existential and geopolitical questions such as: Can it rely on promises made by the Sunni axis led by Turkey? Can this axis guarantee a sustainable interim solution? Failing to respond positively to the regional initiative on the Palestinian issue could isolate Israel and leave it alone in a hostile environment without any allies or support. It is for this reason that one has to study carefully the nature of the coming Sunni axis. A hostile Sunni axis might push Israel into the corner, while a more moderate Sunni axis that adopts the Arab Initiative could assist in stabilizing the region and promoting an interim solution between Israel and Palestine. In a situation of deliberation and a foregoing of the two options, it is possible that Israel will be ready to cautiously move towards an interim agreement with interim borders, while carefully monitoring and examining the results. Stability in neighboring countries would allow the governments of Israel and the Palestinian Authority to overcome those who oppose peace, negotiate and reach an agreement on interim borders without resolving the basic conflict. In this way, they could reach a partial agreement which is supported by the Sunni axis.

Progress towards an agreement of this kind is essential for the Sunni axis. Israel's isolation could push it to forge other alliances. While this seems currently unacceptable, Israel and Iran may reconsider their relationship in the future, especially in light of a hostile Sunni axis threatening both of them. The United

States may also reconsider its relations with the Sunni axis, at the center of which is Turkey, if it chooses to assume a radical Islamic ideology. For these reasons, the Sunni axis may moderate its positions and offer Israel a reasonable solution proposal that suits its security interests.

The proposal will be based on Israeli withdrawal to the 1967 borders while leaving wide security margins. The separation barrier along with additional territories under Israeli control could form an interim border map until a permanent solution is reached. According to this scenario, progress towards a solution to the Israeli-Palestinian conflict will be achieved primarily through regional developments, the rise of Turkey to a leading regional position, the rise of pragmatic national-Islamic parties in the Arab world (including the Palestinian Authority) and regional stability. At this point, neither the Israeli nor the Palestinian side will be ready for a final-status solution due to fundamental disputes regarding the core issues: borders, Jerusalem and the refugees. However, the supportive atmosphere in the region will enable moderate progress towards a partial and interim solution. This geopolitical framework would enable both parties to proceed with economic and cultural reform, and in the longer term, even to reach a permanent solution. This scenario is based on the formation of leading blocs in the Middle East that on the one hand threaten Israel, and yet at the same time provide it with significant room for maneuver.

Scenario 3: Anarchy and Defensible Israeli Borders

In the third scenario, defensible borders, the region witnesses many upheavals up to the point of anarchy and uncertainty for a protracted period of time. It is characterized by internal conflicts, competition between countries, instability and the absence of agreements. Several Middle Eastern governments, including Egypt and the Palestinian Authority, become failed states; in other words, regimes that cannot provide security, implement the rule of law and provide basic economic and social services to residents. Within these states lawless-frontier areas emerge that serve as terror outposts for non-state actors. In such a situation, wars break out between countries over territories, frontier-lands and borders, which could deteriorate into broad regional conflict.

The old superpowers – the U.S. and Russia – are colliding over regional influence and control of the region by forging and reestablishing military alliances. Additional superpowers permeate the region, specifically China and India. American power in the region is in decline, especially after its pullout from

Iraq and Afghanistan. Iran benefits the most from America's waning position, and continues to pursue nuclear armament.

Turkey is trying to establish itself as a leading regional superpower, relying on its size, economic power and geographical location. As a result it will find itself competing with Iran for hegemony. Another conflict is taking place between Saudi Arabia and Iran over control of the Persian Gulf. This rivalry also has religious features: friction between Sunnis and Shi'ites. Confrontations break out from time to time in countries in which there is a large Shi'ite minority, such as Bahrain and Lebanon. The conflict between Israel and Turkey will worsen as the latter pursues its goal of becoming a dominant power in the Middle East. This could deteriorate into significant hostilities and confrontations between Turkish and Israeli forces, which would severely damage NATO and may threaten American and Western interests in the region.

Under such conditions, the superpowers may intervene in an effort to calm down tensions and warn the two parties against further escalation. The purpose of intervention would be to guarantee the superpowers' interests in the Middle East, especially the supply of energy and their hold over strategic areas. Other superpowers may do just the opposite, namely increasing tensions in order to strengthen their influence. China, in cooperation with Iran, may support entities looking to undermine the regime in Saudi Arabia and subsequently America's standing.

Friction between nation-states in this scenario will grow deeper. One of the main sources of conflict between countries is the issue of water. Constant population growth in the Middle East, the rising demand for water and the shortage in its supply will amplify the friction. Turkey, Iraq and Syria will fight over access to the Tigris, Euphrates and Orontes Rivers; Egypt, Ethiopia and Sudan over the Nile; and Israel, Jordan, Syria and Lebanon over the Jordan and Yarmouk rivers; Israel and the Palestinian Authority over the mountain aquifer. Additional clashes may arise over oil and gas pipelines. Repeated damage to the gas pipelines from Egypt to Israel and Jordan and the termination of Egypt's supply of gas to Israel are examples of what could take place in the future.

In this scenario of anarchy, nation-states are consumed by many internal conflicts that have no bearing on the Israeli-Palestinian conflict, such as tribal wars, conflicts between ethno-national minorities, between religious groups and between political and cultural groups with conflicting interests. Tribal conflicts will be especially evident in Iraq, Yemen and Libya. Ethno-national conflicts will include the Kurds in Turkey, the Azeris in Iran, the Alawites in Syria, the Arabs in Israel and the Coptic Christians in Egypt. Bloody confrontations will likely erupt between Shi'ites and Sunnis in Iraq, Saudi Arabia and Bahrain. The conflict between Fatah and Hamas will continue unabated and reconciliation agreements will collapse due to the drive for political and economic power.

Another rivalry is due to arise between democratically oriented secular forces and Islamic forces seeking to impose theocracy. Friction between liberal forces and the Muslim Brotherhood is likely to increase in Egypt. The army's long term position is not clear. One cannot rule out the possibility that it will not remain indifferent to this rivalry as it seeks to maintain its political standing and its economic hold on various enterprises. Iran will have its rivalries between the conservative and reform-oriented forces. Turkey may also experience internal turmoil due to the fragility of its democracy. It is said to have the largest number of incarcerated reporters and its treatment of women is ranked one of the worst in the region. Prime Minister Erdogan's Islamic policy arouses concern among secular Turks and the effort to promote army officers with an Islamic orientation may provoke a counter movement: elements within the army may forge alliances in order to bring about the overthrow of Erdogan and restore the secular tradition reminiscent of Atatürk, the founder of modern Turkey.

A third rivalry that may surface is on the social-political front. This would be especially salient in countries where the Arab Spring blossomed. In the long run it will become clear that the overthrow of authoritarian rulers in Arab countries did not provide a cure for the demographic and economic problems, and that the transition period could go on for quite a while. Once the euphoria surrounding the wave of protests subsides, the hopes the young generation of Arabs put into the revolution will turn out to have been but an illusion. Those that took to the squares ignited the world's imagination, and for a moment it seemed that they would grab the helms of power and bring about a late renaissance to the Arab World. However, in the long run it will become clear that the Arab Spring turned into an autumn or even winter, during which the reins of power were seized by conservative parties like the Muslim Brotherhood, which does not espouse democracy and human rights.

Historical precedents indeed demonstrate that the era of democratic elections in Muslim countries brought about the rise of Islamic regimes hostile to democracy: This was the situation in Iran in 1979 and in the Palestinian Authority in 2006, when Hamas was elected to power. The Muslim Brotherhood's election to parliament in Egypt will not be taken lightly by the young liberal generation or by the Coptic community. A long process of transition from autocratic to democratic power can be expected, including many confrontations. It is important to remember that in Eastern European countries, the transition to democracy was a slow one, and one cannot rule out the possibility that the transition in Muslim countries might be more complicated and more violent.

The results for Egypt could be extremely harsh. The new regime might collapse under the economic burden and political pressures, and even find it difficult to guarantee personal and social safety. This is already apparent in the Sinai Peninsula, where terror groups are setting up bases, occasionally blowing up the oil pipeline leading to Israel and Jordan, threatening travelers in Sinai, killing Egyptian soldiers, firing missiles at Israeli communities and severely damaging Egypt's economy. The Egyptian regime, which is interested in its own survival, is likely to submit to anti-Israel sentiments in the hope that that will bolster its position.

The internal rivalries and the continued armament with conventional and unconventional weapons at the expense of economic and social development may lead to economic collapse in several countries, including Egypt and Syria. There is also the possibility that several countries in the region may become failed states, and that conventional and unconventional weapons will fall into the hands of terror organizations and non-state entities.

The result of such external and internal rivalries is ongoing anarchy in the Middle East, much like the old Balkan model, which calls for international intervention. Such intervention may come from superpowers interested in expanding their power by supporting a specific country or a faction in that country. Possible candidates include Russia, which seeks to restore its geopolitical influence, or China, which is looking to seize energy resources in order to ensure its continued economic growth. Such intervention will include the supply of weapons in exchange for energy and geostrategic influence. Under such an umbrella, Arab countries bordering Israel may choose to attack it or support radical groups operating against it in order to relieve internal political pressures. In such a context, peace between Israel and the Palestinian Authority would hardly influence the situation. The only powers that could affect the anarchic situation in the Middle East and stabilize the region are outside forces, chief among them the U.S.

On-going anarchy in the region will deepen the political and psychological split regarding a permanent resolution, in both Israel and the Palestinian Authority. The governments are declaring their willingness to promote a two-state solution, but are not willing to take the risks necessary for finding a permanent solution. This is because they believe that the risks loom higher than the benefits associated with the agreement. In the same vein, while the public on both sides has expressed support for a two-state solution, it still does not believe the other side can be trusted. Instability in the region is bound to intensify this political and psychological split, thereby thwarting any territorial concessions by Israel. This trend will only strengthen as the radical Shi'ite axis supports radical elements in the Arab world, including Hamas and Hezbollah.

Such unstable regional conditions between Israel and the Palestinian Authority could foster several developments regarding future borders. One possibility is the continuation of the status quo. Without reliable international or regional guarantees, and in light of increased regional chaos, Israel has no substitute for strategic depth provided by the maintenance of existing borders.[65] Another possibility is that both governments will decide that they can take advantage of the regional uncertainty and reach an agreement, even if partial, in order to avoid getting swept up in regional anarchy. Israel will be concerned about the collapse of the Palestinian Authority due to such regional anarchy, which would turn the West Bank into a volatile and threatening frontier area that lacks the authority to impose rule of law. The Palestinian Authority will seek to maintain its political control, even at the price of abandoning the dream of a state along the 1967 borders, and instead settle for interim borders. Political extremism will be replaced by political sobriety. If both regimes turn to sober leadership, an interim agreement over interim borders would be reached in which Israel would withdraw from some of the territories deep in the West Bank and reposition itself within defensible borders.

A third possibility is a unilateral Israeli withdrawal to defensible borders. Such a move would be taken due to Israel's concerns that increased regional anarchy and the collapse of the Palestinian Authority could leave it as the only entity responsible for the West Bank. Such responsibility will obligate Israel to allocate resources, infrastructure and services, and in the long term – basic rights. A West Bank under Israeli sovereignty may turn into a Trojan horse that drags Israel into a binational state. Under such conditions, Israel would prefer to withdraw to defensible borders and unilaterally evacuate settlements deep in the West Bank, in order preserve its character as a Jewish and democratic state.

---

[65] Richard Haass formulated the immutable borders scenario resulting from regional anarchy. See: Haass, July 6, 2011.

Scenario 4: Clash of Civilizations and Blurred Borders

In this scenario, rivalries in the Middle East are expected to intensify and affect other regions, eventually deteriorating into a global war between Islam and the West. Such a development is hard to imagine at a time when the world is becoming more interconnected through processes of globalization and the information revolution. Currently, there is a widespread belief in economic growth, social change and the spread of democracy. A clash of civilizations scenario starkly contradicts these expectations. It projects a radical upheaval in the first half of the 21st century, at the center of which is a religious confrontation between Islam and the West. How could this happen? What could be the driving mechanism?

The driving force in this scenario is the West's retreat from the Middle East and the emergence of radical Islam as a leading regional power. The first signs of such a turn of events can already be detected in the region: The sanctions against Iran and its international isolation, the EU refusal to accept Turkey as a member state, Iranian leaders' threats against Israel and the West, the political transformation in Arab countries and the rise to power of Islamic parties, and finally threats made by Turkey's Prime Minister against Cyprus and Israel. In the long term, Turkey may give up on its efforts to become part of the West and instead choose to focus on the Middle East by developing a geopolitical axis that can compete with the Western world. Such an axis would comprise Muslim countries headed by Turkey and would include Iran.

These developments, which are dependent on alliances between Muslim countries headed by Iran and Turkey, seem unimaginable at the beginning of the 21st century. The two countries are run by Muslim parties that are fundamentally different, one being radical and the other moderate. Iran openly calls for the destruction of Israel, while Turkey is interested in promoting peace in the region. Moreover, a long history of tension and conflict between Sunnis and Shi'ites seems to indicate that the option for an Iranian-Turkish alliance is not likely. Nonetheless, such an option should not be ruled out. Turkey, which requires energy sources located in Iran, has chosen to strengthen its economic and political relations with the latter, to the chagrin of the U.S. Furthermore, Turkey, together with Brazil and Venezuela, refused to support sanctions against Iran in the Security Council, and sought ways to facilitate the continued development of Iranian nuclear weapons. Relations between Turkey and Iran have been improving due to their joint struggle against the Kurdish minority in their countries as well as their opposition to Israel. The fact that Islamic governments are leading both countries may assist in strengthening that alliance. In the long run, the cloak of moderate Islam in which Turkey has wrapped itself may turn out to have been an illusion.

The strengthening of relations between Turkey and Iran is further supported by developments in other Arab and Muslim countries. The Arab Spring is constantly turning into an Arab winter during which Muslim parties– at the forefront of which is the Muslim Brotherhood – are tightening their grip on power. When the dust settles, it will become apparent that fundamentalist Islamic parties rose to power in Tunisia, Egypt, Syria and Yemen.

The rise of these parties signals the dawn of a more dangerous Middle East. The Muslim Brotherhood's power in Egypt is bound to strengthen its ties to Hamas in Gaza, which originally sprang out of it. The cold peace with Israel will become increasingly frigid. The Turkish example of severing relations with Israel will become a popular model emulated by Egypt and Jordan. Once ties are severed, both countries will reconsider their peace treaties with Israel and further strengthen ties with Turkey. All these factors will bolster Hamas, and the refusal to recognize Israel, to honor the Oslo Accords and to abandon terror will find approval in the region. Turkey will explicitly support Hamas and join Iran in its condemnation of Israel and its diplomatic and military antagonism towards it.

The attempt by Western superpowers to calm the tensions between Turkey and Israel will fail. Shortly after it will become clear that the deterioration of relations with Israel and Turkey's demand for an apology were just a cover for a profoundly calculated decision to dismantle the strategic pact between Ankara and Jerusalem and instead ally with Iran, Egypt and Syria. Closer ties with Tehran and support for Hamas will allow the Turkish government to increase its strategic influence in the Middle East as it becomes a dominant power. The regional alliance between Turkey and Iran could create an axis that not only threatens the Middle East, but also countries in neighboring regions, such as Europe and Asia. Such an axis would have military might that includes conventional and unconventional weapons (an "Islamic bomb," according to Samuel Huntington), and possibly benefit from the backing of Pakistan and North Korea. Such an Islamic axis is bound to threaten Israel and the West.

The conflict could eventually deteriorate to war. An Israeli attack on the nuclear facilities in Iran could ignite the region and lead to a world war. An Israeli attack on the Gaza Strip in reaction to terror acts could push Egypt – and as a result other Arab countries – into the geopolitical sphere of Turkey and Iran and ignite a regional war.[66] A wide-scale barrage of missiles on Israel by Hezbollah and Hamas, encouraged by Iran, could draw harsh reaction from Israel, which would in turn be met with a severe reaction from Iran and Turkey. This confrontation could quickly spread to adjacent regions. One cannot rule out the possibility of the rise of a radical government in Pakistan that might choose to join this axis. Such an axis will rely on economic power and have the capability to recruit large swaths of the Muslim population on the basis of religious, anti-Western and anti-Israel sentiments.

These changes may threaten the position of the U.S., the EU and Russia in the region, resulting in their intervention in order to guarantee the supply of oil and control of strategic regions. It is possible that the U.S. and the EU – with the support of Russia – will operate against the crystallizing Islamic alliance, while China may support it in an effort to ensure its supply of economic resources. All these factors contribute to the possibility of a war of civilizations. While this scenario may seem distant, it should not be ruled out, especially in light of the rise to power of Islamic parties in Iran, Turkey, Tunisia, Yemen, Egypt and possibly Syria as well.

This is a disconcerting situation, not just for Israel, but also for the superpowers. Under such circumstances, the U.S., Russia and the EU can be expected to confront the changes in the Middle East and view them as a strategic threat, both militarily and economically. Anxiety over such changes will trickle down to Russia, which is concerned about the strengthening of the Islamic axis on its southern border. This could prompt Russia to increase its ties to the West and to Israel. Israel is bound to be pulled into the Western-Russian framework and be seen as a frontline in the clash of civilizations between Judeo-Christianity and Confucianism and Islamism. It will be one of the only Western islands in the region and its ties to NATO will increase.

In a situation of religious radicalization in Arab countries and the risk of falling into a clash of civilizations, it is improbable that Israel will initiate any changes to its existing borders. Israel will claim that it requires strategic depth that can prevent the invasion of hostile forces into neighboring territories, due to the concrete threat from the Islamic axis and growing concern about a large-scale war. Israel will thus maintain its control over the West Bank and reoccupy the Gaza Strip and even parts of the Sinai Peninsula, while expelling some

---

[66] This paragraph was written about a year before Israel's Pillar of Defense operation in Gaza on November, 2012.

Palestinians, both militant and civilian populations, to hostile countries in the East and the West.

The widespread tendency is to claim that this scenario is impossible. However, many factors in the region prove that it should not be ruled out: Turkey's exasperation with trying to join the EU; the strategic turning point in Turkish policies; the annulment of the strategic alliance with Israel; the endorsement of Hamas; support for Muslim opposition forces in Syria; and the increased affinity with Iran to the chagrin of the U.S.

Additional signs include: Iran's determination to develop nuclear weapons despite sanctions imposed by Western countries; the rise of the Muslim Brotherhood to power in Egypt and Tunisia; the transformation of the Sinai Peninsula into an anarchic breeding ground for terrorists; and the sharpening tensions between Israel and Erdogan's Islamic government. On the other hand, there are also indications of growing security cooperation between Israel and European countries, including Greece, Romania, Bulgaria and increased cooperation between Israel and NATO. These signs all indicate that an Islamic civilization in the Middle East is crystallizing, and thus triggering heightened tensions with the West.

These signs are being perceived in a compartmentalized way by Israel, not as part of a complete strategic paradigm. The establishment of the Hamas government; hostility towards Israel in Egypt and Jordan; terror attacks originating in Sinai; heightened tensions with Turkey; explicit threats by Iran and Turkey, Palestinian insistence on shunning negotiations with Israel - these all contribute to the notion in Israel that there is no partner to talk to and nothing to talk about. The perpetuation of the status quo in terms of geopolitics means borders stretching along the Jordan River and the containment within Israel of a large and hostile Palestinian minority with no political rights. This constitutes a threat to Israel's character as a Jewish and democratic state, and in the long term undermines its social and moral fortitude.

CONCLUSION: ISRAEL'S GEOPOLITICAL DILEMMA IN THE MIRROR OF THE DIFFERENT SCENARIOS

Each one of the scenarios presents a distinct solution to Israel's geopolitical dilemma. The most agreeable scenario is an "American peace" and a permanent solution on the basis of the 1967 borders. This scenario will assure Israel a large measure of national homogeneity, fortification of a democratic regime throughout the country within the framework of secure borders and the attainment of regional and international legitimacy. This is the most comprehensive solution to Israel's geopolitical dilemma as it has been presented in this paper.

The major problem is that the Middle East is undergoing changes contrary to the trends described in this scenario. It is therefore unlikely that it will be realized in the near future. The U.S. is attempting to promote regional stability through dialogue with the Islamic parties in the Arab world, and is leading the opposition to Iran. However it is highly unlikely that the Islamic parties will adopt a moderate policy on Israel. It appears as though the aspiration of the Arab world – including both Islamic and secular elements within it - to wipe Israel off the map is not going to disappear.

On the regional level, it appears that Turkey and Iran are working to limit American influence in the Middle East. The explicit decline of U.S power is evident, among other factors, due to its withdrawal from Iraq; the subsequent strengthening of ties between Iraq and Iran; American inability to prove victorious in Afghanistan; in its rising conflict with Pakistan; and its failure to get Israel on a negotiation track. All these factors are strengthening regional forces in the area that directly oppose the U.S. It is possible that an American attack on Iran will reverse these trends and strengthen the chances for a new regional order in the Middle East. However, it appears that in the foreseeable future, the trends are ones of deterioration and escalation in the region. As long as the Middle East is a hostile and dangerous place, Israel will have no incentive to reach a permanent solution on the basis of 1967 borders. On the other hand, Israeli interests necessitate maximum cooperation with the U.S. in an effort to stabilize the region. This has created a situation of mutual dependency between the strengthening of America's positioning on a regional level, and a solution to the Israeli-Palestinian conflict on a local level. This situation is not devoid of risks; however it is the best long-term option.

The Islamic Caliphate scenario contains both risks and opportunities for Israel. The scenario guarantees regional stability in one of two ways: a balance of power between the Sunni axis led by Turkey and the Shi'ite axis led by Iran, or Turkish hegemony. In both cases, Israel would need to maneuver between allies and adversaries in the region. In a situation of a balance of power, Israel may be sought-after by both camps. A situation of Turkish hegemony would allow Israel to consider joining the Turkish camp on condition that it recognizes the superiority of Turkey in the region and operates according to its rules. Remaining within the existing borders will be interpreted as a refusal to accept the Turkey's conditions and lead to Israel's increased isolation in the Middle East and to confrontations with a broad and cohesive Sunni camp.

In both cases – hegemony or balance of power – Israel will be required to prove its good will and readiness to fulfill the conditions set by leaders of this camp. This means that even if an agreement with the Palestinians is not attained directly, Israel will need to rely on regional mediators and grant concessions to the Palestinians by withdrawing to interim borders. This will allow Israel to attain regional legitimacy, bolster its national homogeneity and advance its democratic structures.

The "Anarchy" scenario has a high likelihood of being realized. This is the business-as-usual scenario. Regional anarchy feeds off of several sources: demographic growth and economic problems, tribal, religious and social fragmentation, secular-religious confrontations and the absence of a government powerful enough to cope with these problems. This scenario of instability due to internal and regional conflicts is bound to continue for a long time, and could even turn into an all-out war.

The anarchy scenario seemingly enables Israel to remain in its current situation, namely, maintaining its existing borders. However, in a state of anarchy in which the Palestinian Authority may collapse, Israel is better off withdrawing to defensible borders: a security border in the east and a political border in the west, ideally through an agreement with the PA, and if not, then unilaterally. If Israel does not take these steps, it will be forced to reassume responsibility for the Palestinian population, which will be bereft of any administrative political body. This would not only damage Israel's notion of national homogeneity, but also the state's democratic character, as well as its international standing. Within the framework of the anarchy scenario, Israel will be able to take advantage of the instability and the fact that Arab countries are preoccupied with their internal issues in order to reorganize itself – withdrawing to defensible borders – without the concern about a substantial external threat.

The "Clash of Civilizations" scenario seems incomprehensible. It contradicts the currently prevailing notions of progress, modernization and globalization. Nonetheless, a deeper examination of the processes taking place in the Middle East indicates a reinforcement of Islam as well as a trend of religious movements across national boundaries. Iran is invested in many of the countries in the region and has set its sights on the Persian Gulf's oil resources. Turkey is building ties with Iran and with countries like Egypt, Syria (by supporting opposition forces), Libya and the Hamas government in Gaza. Turkey's failed attempt to join the EU is pushing it to establish itself as a regional power in the Middle East. Turkey may choose to adopt a reckless policy if it joins forces with Iran. It is hard to imagine that Israel will face such an Islamic union alone and it is likely that superpowers will intervene, primarily to secure their own economic and strategic interests in the region.

It is improbable that Israel will be pressured by the West to concede territory in such a situation. During a time of war, territorial depth is highly critical, especially to prevent the invasion of hostile armies into territories from which they can threaten Israel. It is likely that Israel will retain control of the West Bank, strengthen its ties to the West and be isolated in the Middle East. If and when an all-out war erupts, Israel will not be alone; however the risks posed by a war of this scale are higher than anything Israel has ever known. The dangers posed to the Jewish majority in the country, its democratic structure and its moral character will all significantly increase.

The picture that emerges from a comprehensive examination of all the scenarios is that, with the exception of the "American Peace" scenario, Israel is destined to find itself increasingly isolated in the region. The major driving force on a local level is the religious-national one and it is associated with anti-Israel sentiments. On a regional level, the driving force is the determination to enhance strategic importance and economic power by forming alliances. This goal views Israel as an economic and strategic threat. Such forces are acting against Israel since they see it as a rival and even an enemy. There is no guarantee that an Israeli-Palestinian agreement can put an end to such strategic desires, which are not related to Israel. These desires reflect a geopolitical tendency to assume control of energy sources, strategic paths and positions of power in the Middle East, and consequently view Israel's power as a threat. Iran never took an interest in Palestinians, and Turkey was allied with Israel for many years despite Israel's control of the West Bank.

These regional changes will affect decisions taken by both the Palestinian and Israeli governments. It is safe to assume that as threats to Israel increase, so will the Israeli aversion to territorial concessions. The cognitive dissonance characterizing Israeli public opinion will deepen. Today, the majority of the Israeli public supports a two-state solution but does not trust the Palestinian and therefore is not willing to make territorial concessions. In the future, the increased threats will contribute to a deeper lack of trust among Israelis, and the Middle East as a whole will be viewed with suspicion. . The downgrading of diplomatic relations, threats of annulling the peace treaties or their actual annulment, will radicalize Israeli positions further. Israel's isolation in the region will lead superpowers to pressure Israel to apologize, retreat, and lower its profile. This could prove in the long run a dangerous precedent that bolsters the aggressor.

In the long term, it is in Israel's interest to withdraw to 1967 borders with land swaps, in order to create a more homogenous nation-state. This is President Obama's vision, and should shape Israel's long-term policy. Middle East upheaval points to the need for fresh strategic thinking on the regional level. Such thinking must include regional security, cultural changes and economic potential, and be able to provide guarantees for a permanent agreement between Israel and the Palestinian Authority. What is needed is a stable Middle East, unwavering democratic countries and a strong and united Palestinian Authority. It is only under such conditions that Israelis and Palestinians can reach an agreement regarding the core issues of borders, Jerusalem and refugees. As long as these conditions are absent, it is difficult to expect any progress towards an agreement on the basis of the 1967 borders, at the center of which is two states for two peoples.

Fostering a stable Middle East, in which peace can be achieved between Israel, Palestinians and the Arab world, requires the management of deep and challenging problems. These problems – which include cultural tensions, national hostilities, regional rivalries over power and global interests in energy sources and strategic paths – contribute to making the Middle East an incendiary place that is liable to ignite at any moment. This fragile atmosphere could send the price of oil up and threaten the stability of the markets. If tensions deepen and lead to confrontations between central forces in the region – Iran Turkey, Israel and Egypt – this could not only endanger the region but the entire world. The weapons possessed by the different sides, including non-conventional weapons, may cause such an eruption to spread from the region to neighboring countries and even the rest of the world.

Such a situation calls for leaders with a comprehensive strategic approach that takes into account aspects of security, economy, and culture, which all threaten to undermine regional peace. Without coping with these issues, it will be difficult to solve Israel's geopolitical dilemma. The kind of leadership that navigated through WWII is needed: Roosevelt, Churchill and Stalin. Unfortunately the international and regional leadership presiding over an increasingly volatile Middle East that faces global, regional and national threats does not have the skills necessary to deal with the reality.

Israeli leadership will have to cope with the geopolitical changes taking place on the various levels – global, regional, inter-Arab, Palestinian-Israeli and Israeli – and prepare itself for a protracted conflict that involves economic, political, cultural and security-related components.

1. On the global level, Israel should tread cautiously amid changes in the balance of power among superpowers and examine their consequences for the region. The option of American detachment from Israel should be taken into account, due to shifts in the geopolitical center of gravity to Southeast Asia and the bleak outlook for peace in the Middle East. Israel's increasing international isolation should also be taken into account as far as its implications on the global level. Furthermore, Russia's desire to reassume a central geopolitical role in the region – among other things, through supporting Iran and Syria – should not be dismissed.

2. On the regional level, Israel should prepare itself for changes, including the emergence of new coalitions and powers. Israel will be forced to confront a nuclear Iran, an increasingly dominant Turkey seeking power by weakening Israel, and unprecedented actions carried out by Iran's proxies in the region. In this context, non-state entities should also be taken into consideration; entities that enjoy military intelligence, training, funding and advanced weapons from Iran. An alliance between Iran and Turkey will present Israel with a severe security challenge and force it to engage in supra-regional geopolitical thinking.

3. On the inter-state level, Israel must prepare for the changes bound to take place in the Arab world as a result of the Arab Spring. These include economic, political and cultural transformations and the long process of transition from an autocratic regime to a more democratic one. The most visible threat from such processes is the rise to power of Islamic-nationalist regimes that are hostile to Israel.

4. On the bilateral level regarding relations with the Palestinian Authority, Israel should prepare for changes in the PA in light of the deep cultural and political divide between the West Bank and Gaza and the risk of the PA's collapse. Continued fragmentation will make an agreement less likely and necessitate the devising of a different approach. Any agreement signed with the authority governing the West Bank will be meaningless in light of the rejection by the government in Gaza, which enjoys the support of regional forces that are hostile to Israel. On the other hand, the collapse of the PA could leave Israel with the West Bank but without a partner. The rise of Hamas to power would place Israel in a difficult geopolitical position and require new approaches regarding its relations with the PA, including its ability to reach an interim agreement.

5. On the internal level, Israel must pay attention to the deepening social divisions in its society and the risks involved in remaining in the Occupied Territories and becoming a de facto bi-national state. The deep split in Israeli society regarding an agreement with the PA could get worse and express itself in violent ways, which are already evident from actions known as "price tags" and settler violence towards Israeli soldiers. The continuation of these processes could threaten the current state of affairs and Israel's existence as a Jewish and democratic state that abides by the rule of law.

The processes are taking place on these five levels at different paces. It is difficult to estimate where the first crisis will occur. At the time of writing, it appears that processes on the regional and global levels are proceeding at a faster pace. At this stage, it is also clear that the Israeli-Palestinian conflict is not the cause of regional and global tensions in the Arab world. Those reasons are more profound and are related to extensive geo-strategic, political, cultural and economic processes. Iran is blatantly threatening Israel, in ways akin to the threats of annihilation by the Nazis. Turkey has been condemning Israel in unprecedented ways and the rise of extreme national-religious regimes in Arab countries does not bode well. As a result of these developments, the Israeli-Palestinian conflict has become secondary, and with that the opportunity to settle Israel's geopolitical dilemma once and for all. The internal divisions among both Palestinians and Israelis reduce the chances for a permanent resolution and instead propagate the status quo: the manifestation of a de facto bi-national state.

In light of these developments, what the majority of the Israeli public wants – a Jewish and democratic nation-state – is impossible. On the other hand, remaining in the Occupied Territories and the eventual manifestation of a bi-national state – what most Israelis oppose – seems far more plausible. There are two opposing approaches that have emerged as a way to break the deadlock. One approach sees the way out through Tehran – in other words, without a regional solution there can be no local solution. The second approach, embraced by Western countries, says the opposite: the road to Tehran passes through Jerusalem – that is, without a local solution there can be no regional solution. Both solutions simplify a complex situation and promise unrealistic and dangerous solutions. The belief that the road to Jerusalem goes through Tehran could prove the most dangerous. Continuing to push for it could eternalize the status quo of Israel's control over the Palestinian population and even lead to a regional war that could turn into a world war. The belief that the way to Tehran runs through Jerusalem is also risky, since it could lead to an Israeli withdrawal to borders that could endanger the entire country.

What seems to be needed under these conditions is a creative political approach that searches for new solutions to be found somewhere between the two poles outlined. Israel must be proactive in leading new political processes, while remaining aware of the fact that the turmoil threatening the Middle East is inestimably worse than the local Israeli-Palestinian conflict. Under the current circumstances, retreating to the 1967 borders is unfeasible due to security considerations; however, as has been demonstrated, the status quo is not an option either.

Israel should thus adopt a geopolitical approach that allows it to break the walls of international isolation, to further strengthen its relationship with the U.S. and improve its standing in the region. Israel should propose a bold political initiative regarding its conflict with the Palestinians that will enjoy international support, out of an understanding that in terms of geopolitics, the main threat is not from the Palestinians, but rather from the international, regional, and local changes taking place in the Muslim and Arab world.

Israel should prepare for a political initiative in accordance with the regional anarchy and Islamic caliphate scenarios, since these are the most likely ones. The two scenarios point to a threat of confrontation, but also chart the option of temporary calm. In both scenarios, Israel can maintain its existing borders; however, that will lead to local clashes that could become regional and thus chill relations with the U.S. It is therefore precisely because the anarchy and Islamic caliphate scenarios are most likely to happen, that Israel should adopt a policy of withdrawing to interim borders or to defensible borders. Both strategies are similar, since they each provide progress towards a solution to the Israeli-

Palestinian conflict and to the improvement of Israel's geopolitical standing, without having reached a permanent solution. This interim solution can provide both sides with many advantages that allow for a non-combative situation. It will not put an end to ideological ambitions, and will provide the time needed for paradigm shift towards a final-status solution.

SOURCES (Hebrew)

Arieli, Shaul. *Going for "All" Leaving with Nothing: Approaches in the struggle over the State of Israel's borders.* Jerusalem, Carmel: 2006.

Benn, Aluff. "Wikileaks Documents: Leaked with the Wind." *Haaretz*, December 3, 2010.

Caspit, Ben. "Dr. Ehud and Mr. Barak: The two faces of the Defense Minister" *Ma'ariv*, July 31, 2010.

Galnoor, Itzhak. "The polemic over the partition plan and borders during the Mandate." Ruth Gavison (Ed.) *60 Years to the November 29th 1947 Resolution.* Jerusalem: Metzilah Center for Zionist, Jewish Liberal and Humanist Thought, p. 27-48.

Ginzburg, Ami. "What will happen to oil shares if Ahmadinejad closes the Straits of Hormuz?" *The Marker, Haaretz,* January 29, 2012.

Hasson, Shlomo, Ben-Bassat, Avraham, Halevy, Ephraim, Neeman, Uri, Newman, David, Sabel, Robbie; Sela, Avraham, Feitelson, Eran. *The Future borders between Israel and the Palestinian Authority: principles Scenarios and Recommendations.* Jerusalem: Hebrew University of Jerusalem, Shasha Center for Strategic Studies, Federman School of Public Policy and Government , 2011.

Lindenstrauss, Gallia. "Turkey and the Middle East: Between Euphoria and Sobriety." http://www.inss.org.il/upload/(FILE)1316602631.pdf

Magen, Zvi and Bagno-Moldavsky, Olena. "New directions in Russian foreign policy: Implications for the Middle East." *Strategic Assessment,* Volume 13: No. 4, January 2011, p. 65-75.

Meital, Yoram. Egypt: A shock-absorbing policy. In: *Strategic Assessment for Israel 2010.* Shlomo Brom, Anat Kurz, (Eds.), Institute for National Security Studies, Tel Aviv University, p. 151-162.

Netanyahu, Benjamin. *A Place in the Sun.* Tel Aviv: Miskal Yedioth Ahronoth and Hemed Books, 2001.

Schueftan, Dan. *Disengagement: Israel and the Palestinian Entity.* Haifa: University of Haifa Press and Zmora Bitan, 1999.

Shenhav, Yehuda. *In the Trap of the Green Line: Jewish Political Mass.* Tel Aviv: Am Oved, 2010.

Soffer, Arnon and Pollack, Karen. *Israel's unilateral separation from the Palestinian Authority: Advantages and disadvantages.* Haifa: Geostrategy Katedra, National Security Studies Center, University of Haifa, 2003.

Stein, Shimon. The European Union and the Middle East. In: *Strategic Assessment for Israel 2010*. Shlomo Brom, Anat Kurz, (Eds.), Institute for National Security Studies, Tel Aviv University, p. 137-150.

Zeitun, Yoav. "Defense Ministry cancels deal with Turkey" *Ynet*, December 12, 2011. http://www.ynet.co.il/articles/0,7340,L-4165695,00.html

SOURCES (English)

Ajami, Fouad. 2012 . "The Arab Spring At One." *Foreign Affairs*, January 24. http://www.foreignaffairs.com/articles/137053/fouad-ajami/the-arab-spring-at-one

Allon, Yigal. 1976. "Israel: The Case for Defensible Borders," *Foreign Affairs*, **55**, 40:38–53.

Aras, Bulent and Ozbay, Fatih. 2008. "The limits of the Russian-Iranian strategic alliance: its history and geopolitics, and the nuclear issue". Korea Institute for Defense Analyses, http://www.informaworld.com

Arens, Moshe, "Israeli Citizenship to Palestinians," *Haaretz*, June 2, 2010. http://www.haaretz.com/print-edition/opinion/is-there-another-option-1.293670

Avineri, Shlomo. July 4, 2008. "What Cyprus, Bosnia, and Kosovo Can Teach Us," *Haaretz*, www.haaretz.com/print-edition/opinion/what-cyprus-bosnia-and-kosovo-can-teach-us-1.249091

Benvenisti, Meron, "The Binationalism Vogue," *Haaretz*, April 4, 2009 http://www.haaretz.com/print-edition/opinion/the-binationalism-vogue-1.275085

Brzezinski, Zbigniew and Scowcroft, Brent. 2008. *America and the World: Conversations on the Future of American Foreign Policy*. New York: Basic Books.

Cagaptay, Soner. 2010. "Sultan of the Muslim world," *Foreign Affairs*, November, http://www.foreignaffairs.com/articles/67009/soner-cagaptay/sultan-of-the-muslim-world

Clinton, Hillary. November 2011. America's Pacific century. *Foreign Policy* http://www.foreignpolicy.com/articles/2011/10/11/americas_pacific_century

Cohen, Saul Bernard. 2009. *Geopolitics: The Geography of International Relations*. Lanham and Plymouth, Rowman and Littlefield Publishers.

Commission of the European Communities. 2004. *European Neighbourhood Policy: Strategy Paper.*

DellaPergola, Sergio. 2011. *Jewish demographic Policies: Population Trends and Options in Israel and in the Diaspora*. The Jewish People Policy Institute. http://jppi.org.il/uploads/Jewish_Demographic_Policies.pdf

Economist. February 11th 2012. "Israel and Iran: Closer to Take-Off".

Ezzat, Dina. 29 September – 5 October, 2011. "Four Middle East scenarios." *Al-Ahram, Weekly-Online.* http://weekly.ahram.org.eg/2011/1066/eg1.htm

Eizenstat Stuart E. Forthcoming. *Uncharted Waters.* http://jppi.org.il/uploads/Uncharted_Waters.pdf

European Commission. 2011. *A new response to a changing neighborhood: A review of European neighbourhood policy.* http://ec.europa.eu/world/enp/pdf/com_11_303_en.pdf

Ferguson, Niall. 2004. *Colossus: The Rise and Fall of the American Empire.* London: Allen Lane.

Friedman, George. 2011. *The Next Decade.* New York: Doubleday.

Haass Richard, N. July 6, 2011. "The Arab Spring Has Given Way to a Long, Hot Summer." http://www.cfr.org/middle-east/arab-spring-has-given-way-long-hot-summer/p25426

Hasson, Shlomo. 2010. "Israel's Geopolitical Dilemma." *Euroasian Geography and Economics,* Vol. LI, No.6. pp. 694-715.

Heller, Joseph. 2000. *The Birth of Israel, 1945-1949: Ben-Gurion and His Critics,* Gainesville: University Press of Florida.

Herzl, Theodor. [1902] 1960. *Altneuland: Old-New Land,* Haifa,: Haifa Pub. Co..

Hider, James, "Palestinian Prime Minister Salam Fayyad Says Time Is Running out for Peace," *The Times,* August 25, 2009. http://www.timesonline.co.uk/tol/news/world/middle_east/article6808557.ece

Hilal, Jamil. 2007. *Where Now for Palestine?: The Demise of the Two-State Solution*: Zed Books.

Jabotinsky, Zeev. 1948. "Zeev Jabotinsky's Speech before a Group of Members of the British Parliament, 13 July, 1937" *Writings of Zeev Jabotinsky, Vol V,* Jerusalem: Ari Jabotinksy Publication, 275-287.

Kardas, Saban. October 10, 2011. "Turkey's Middle East Policy Reloaded: Rise of Pragmatism?". The German Marshall Fund of the United States. www.gmfus.org/.../turkeys-emergence-as-a-middle-eastern-stakehold

Khalaf Roula. February 1, 2011. "Three scenarios for Arab world's trendsetter," *Financial Times.*

Lesser, I.O. Nardulli, B.R., and Arghavan, L.A. 1998. "Sources of conflict in the Middle East." In: In: Zalmay Khalilzad, Ian O. Lesser (Eds.). *Sources of conflict in the 21st century.* Rand, pp. 171-229.

Levy Daniel. October 7, 2011. "Will the Real Benjamin Netanyahu Please Stand Up?" *Foreign Policy.* See: http://www.foreignpolicy.com/articles/2011/10/06/bibi_in_a_box

Los Angeles Times, November 1, 2010. "Turkey: Ankara adds Israel to list of strategic security threats." http://latimesblogs.latimes.com/babylonbeyond/2010/11/israel-turkey-iran-threat-politics-war.html

Makovsky David. 13.4.2010. "Obama and Netanyahu can't afford to disagree." *Haaretz*. http://www.haaretz.com/print-edition/opinion/obama-and-netanyahu-can-t-afford-to-disagree-1.284148

Mishal, Shaul and Avraham Sela. 1999. *The Hamas Wind: Violence and Coexistence*. Tel Aviv, Israel: Yedioth Ahronoth and Chemed Books.

Morozova, Natalia. 2009. "Geopolitics, Eurasianism and Russian Foreign Policy Under Putin". *Geopolitics*, 14:667–686.

National Intelligence Council. 2004. *Mapping the Global Futures: Report of the National Intelligence Council's 2020 Project*. http://www.foia.cia.gov/2020/2020.pdf

National Intelligence Council and EU Institute for Security Studies. 2010. *Global Governance 2025: At a Critical Juncture*. http://www.dni.gov/nic/PDF_2025/2025_Global_Governance.pdf

Özel, Soli and Tuğtan, Mehmet Ali. October 12, 2011. How Will the United States Avoid Paralysis with Turkey? The German Marshall Fund of the United States. http://www.gmfus.org/galleries/ct_publication_attachments/Ozel_Tugtan_CarterMoment_Oct11.pdf;jsessionid=ak0h3JXCtVk7tx2x_1

PSR (Palestinian Center for Policy and Survey Research), Survey Research Unit, *Public Opinion Poll #11; Palestinian Opinion Pulse*. Ramallah, West Bank, December 2004.

PSR - Survey Research Unit. 2011. Joint Israeli Palestinian Poll, December.

Palestine Strategy Group. 2011. Towards New Strategies for Palestinian National Liberation. http://www.palestinestrategygroup.ps/Towards_New_Strategies_For_Palestinian_National_Liberation_FINAL_8-2011_(English).pdf

Scham Paul and Abu-Irshaid Osama. 2009. "Hamas: Ideological Rigidity and Political Flexibility". United States Institute of Peace. http://www.usip.org/files/resources/Special%20Report%20224_Hamas.pdf

Shearman Peter. 2009. "Russia, Post-Communist Europe, and the Geopolitics of Eurasia". *The Russian Review* 68 (January 2009): 122–25

Telhami Shibley. 2011. 2011 Arab Public Opinion Survey, University of Maryland. http://www.brookings.edu/~/media/Files/rc/reports/2011/1121_arab_public_opinion_telhami/1121arab_public_opinion.pdf

The White House: Office of Press Secretary. 19 May, 2011. FACT SHEET: "A Moment of Opportunity" in the Middle East and North Africa. http://www.whitehouse.gov/the-press-office/2011/05/19/fact-sheet-moment-opportunity-middle-east-and-north-africa

Walker Joshua W. and Alessandri, Emiliano. October 10, 2011. "Turkey's Emergence as a Middle Eastern: Stakeholder and What this Means for the West." The German Marshall Fund of the United States. www.gmfus.org/.../turkeys-emergence-as-a-middle-eastern-stakehold

Yariv, A. Alpher, J. Feldman, S. Ben-Meir, Y. Ben-Zvi, A. Eytan, Z. Gazit, S. Gold, D. Heller, M. Karsh, E. Kurz, A. Levite, A. Meir, S. Peri, Y. &. Shalev, A.(1989) *The West Bank and Gaza: Israel's Options for Peace*, Report of the JCSS Study Group, Tel Aviv University.